QUIT HO!

"Absurdity and believability collide. In a world with a plethora of turmoil and negativity, *Quit Honking!* is a welcome reprieve. Fergus explores the themes of keeping up, not feeling good enough, and when is enough really enough with humor that kept me deeply connected throughout. It was impossible to predict where each story would take me, which is precisely what made it a page turner. If you don't want to feel good or be happy, don't read this book!"

— Anita McGue, world traveler, avid bicyclist, and reader

"You can't help but smile in pure amusement or pleasant bewilderment while reading this book. This is not your typical story book, thank God! Doug Fergus takes you on a wild ride into his delightfully kooky, freely mischievous, vibrantly personal, and oddly relatable thoughts and imagination with PLENTY of genius wordplay!"

— Jay Jean, actor and screenwriter

augh-out-loud punny! Doug's uninhibited, childlike nature and lingness to go where no writer has gone before makes for a ride."

—Mark Arinsberg, Citizen 44 Podcast

njoyed *Quit Honking!* and found it entertaining. My favorite ts were when it appeared that the author was drawing from sonal experiences. I identified with the frustrations and ggle of acknowledgement for creative expression. Overall, nd it to be a fun and uplifting book."

— Felicity Lynn, multi-media artist

d *Quit Honking!* because I like off the track, different ches in movies and books. I loved the character portray- t poked fun at the obnoxious, self-absorbed feelings of deserving entitlement in American society. I resonated with the subjects of everybody looking for a role in life and the ease of addiction in our society."

— Nick Arre, financial planner

"I really enjoyed reading this collection of humorous stories that gave me many laugh-out-loud moments. This book is filled with funny, quirky characters and absurd events. It was like a crazy, wild ride that went in so many directions and kept me guessing at every turn. I especially enjoyed the author's play on words and clever writing. The author collected the absurd thoughts and behaviors that many of us have experienced. This is a very fun book; you won't regret reading it!"

— Elaine Beraza, retired school superintendent

Praise for
SMALL PORTIONS CAFE

"In his first collection of short stories, *Small Portions Cafe*, Douglas Fergus makes us laugh. A lot. And keeps us on board for the ride. These 'small portions' reveal the instinct—or technique—of a seasoned practitioner of fiction. You could characterize his genre as "stand-up fiction." Fergus's pearls of perception border on keen discernment or wisdom. The ride that Fergus takes us on *seems* to be one rooted in truth—involving a steady growth, not just of humor, but also of humility. Of humanity. Fergus has become who he was supposed to be, all along: quite an author and comedian."
— James B. Nicola, New York stage director and author of six books of poetry

"Even the intro to this book made me laugh. With self-deprecating humor, quick wit, (infinite parenthetical asides), and a seemingly incorruptible joie de vivre, Doug Fergus tells stories that make me fall in love with being alive—not because life is so great, but because sometimes it's not so great and yet he finds the ways to make it a pleasure. The book is not written as a how-to manual, but it *is* one—how to find joy in unlikely and desperate places. What a gift, this book, to my grumpy self. I loved it."
— Rosemerry Wahtola Trommer, author of 13 poetry collections, writing teacher, speaker, performer

"Common life experiences go through a house of mirrors to become silly, quirky and absurd additions to this short story collection. Each story is well-written, with the setting and character fleshed out enough to make them unique. This collection offers variety that could suit any mood while still working together as a collection. With puns, play on words and the occasional 4th wall break, the author's sense of humour and perspective are clear throughout the book. An entertaining read for those who favour hyperbolic and absurdist humour."
— LoveReading website

"This book was an interesting, fun, and quirky read. Absolutely hilarious! I never thought hypoglycemia, bologna sandwiches, and bedwetting could cause me to laugh so much!"
— Becks, Goodreads reviewer

"*Small Portions Cafe* is a book of short stories that start off as confessional reminiscences then veer off into social satire and surrealism—think of Sedaris-meets-Vonnegut-meets-Firesign Theater. It's full of entertaining wordplay and humorous digressions, with some of the best stories being MOSTLY digressions. This is one of those books that will cause you to say 'ONE more chapter, then I'll go to bed.' It's like buying a bag of really tasty miniature cookies. I highly recommend this hilarious and often heartwarming book."
— Dal Carver was a musician and restaurant owner

QUIT HONKING!

QUIT HONKING!
(I'm Pedaling as Fast as I Can)

DOUGLAS FERGUS

Copyright © 2024 by Douglas Bruce Fergus

All rights reserved. No part of this publication may be reproduced, distributed, or transmitted in any form or by any means, including photocopying, recording, or other electronic or mechanical methods, without the prior written permission of the author, except in the case of brief quotations embodied in critical reviews and certain other noncommercial uses permitted by copyright law.

This book is a work of fiction. Other than actual historical events, people, and places referred to, all names, characters, and incidents are from the author's imagination. Any resemblances to persons, living or dead, are coincidental, and no reference to any real person is intended.

Published by Lucky Doug Press

To contact the author about speaking or bulk orders of this book, visit www.luckydougpress.com.

ISBN (paperback): 978-1-7373198-3-2
ISBN (ebook): 978-1-7373198-4-9

Edited by Jessica Vineyard, Red Letter Editing, Redletterediting.com
Book design by Christy Day, Constellation Book Services
Author photo credit: Barbara Hunt Nazari

Printed in the United States of America

To all the people who go about their daily lives and allow me to watch them through my absurd-colored glasses.

CONTENTS

Introduction	1
Why Are There Awards?	5
Scam Artist	8
Buy My Book	16
Oh, You Silly Words	42
Trance Dance	47
Saint Petra and Her Pearly Gates	53
Quit Honking! (I'm Pedaling as Fast as I Can)	100
Bedroom Remodels	108
Cookies for CorkyLee	111
IndieTop Chart	138
Pull the Lever . . . NOW!	141
The Bushy Brown Beards	146
How to Handle Several Talents	179
Good at Too Many Things	186
I'm Going to Make It! (I Think)	200
America's Got Mediocrity	259
Earn as You Learn	261
Acknowledgments	281
About the Author	282

In your next life, what will you be?
A fish or a tree?
Live carefully.
You may come back as yourself.

—Lucky Doug Fergus
from his song, "In Your Next Life"

INTRODUCTION

Hello, dear reader! Here I am with my second book. My second *album*. My sophomore effort. If you are reading this book (and I suppose you *are* if you are reading this), I thank you very much. (Maybe you also got to enjoy reading my first collection of short stories, *Small Portions Café: A Tempting Assortment of Stories*, available on Amazon and Audible.)

The theme of this collection is summed up quite nicely in the book's title: *Quit Honking! (I'm Pedaling as Fast as I Can)*. You know, it's that sense that we're not good enough, not big enough or strong enough or fast enough or smart enough. We want to keep up with the Joneses and be paid well for the work we do, but why put in the extra effort to rise above? Shouldn't our friends, neighbors, and bosses *see* that we are better than average and treat us accordingly?

We think of ourselves as high achievers, but we're kinda lazy and always want to do things the easy way. In other words, leave me alone. Don't push me. Don't compare me to others. I'm doing the best I can. I'll see you at the "Just Good Enough to Get By" awards ceremony.

With that in mind, I wrote this book over the course of eighteen months, mostly in between chores, tasks, and life events. As a full-time professional wannabe writer, I had to squeeze in time wherever I could. I wrote in Ashland, Oregon; Auburn, California; Telluride, Colorado; Miami, Florida; and Cabarete, Dominican Republic. I tink-tink-tinked with chisel and stone tablet in Georgia, in the cities of Fayetteville, Newnan, Peachtree City, Senoia, and Atlanta.

I wrote in coffee shops, where I pretended I was a famous author and the only reason that people weren't coming up to me was because the delightful staff whispered to each new guest, "Don't look now, shhh! He's *creating*. Yes! That's *him*!" I scrawled during lunch breaks, on airplanes, and in hotels. I even wrote at an old house in Oregon that was a residence for Vladimir Nabokov in the 1950s when he was working on his book *Lolita*! No, wait, that was an HVAC job I did there. Still a true story, just different work.

I scribbled out this entire book on an Apple MacBook Pro, saved it in Google Drive, and sent progress copies to my email. I never once had anything on paper, so I preserved the use of our precious trees for the making of extremely thin paper, on which one can blow one's nose.

I hope you don't take as long to read this book as I did to write it. I also hope that you enjoy reading it as much as I enjoyed writing it, and that if someone honks at you, you will feel free to slow down on the pedaling.

Oh! And be sure to check out my song "If You Don't Do It (Someone Else Will)."

(It's relevant, I promise! My editor wouldn't let me include it in the introduction if it weren't.)

WHY ARE THERE AWARDS?

Why do humans feel the need to hand out awards? There are awards for anything and everything. I'm not typing today about *grades*, which I think are useful to gauge progress, but *awards*, like for being best at something.

Why do we, as a society, have these silly awards? Best cake maker, highest jumper, fastest typist, most cars sold in one month. When did all this start? In caveperson times? Best hunter? Fastest firewood gatherer? Best cave cleaner and cook? Cutest loincloth? Farthest bone thrower? As hideous and unevolved as men were back then, do we all agree there probably was a Fastest Wife Dragger contest? Surely there was an award for the best cave painting!

How about all the stupid awards for movies, TV shows, and music? It's gotten so ridiculous that there are awards for the Best Awards Show.

Opera: Come to Gran Teatro La Fenice in Venice, Italy, to attend the annual OMA show, the Opera Music

Awards! This year we have combined the opera awards with America's country music awards. The event has been renamed the OMA-CMA awards. I wonder who'll win for best soprano, female, and best contralto, male. We also have categories for highest falsetto and longest note held. In the country music portion of the show, who will win for best yodeler? Personally, I'm anxious to find out what group will take home the trophy for best song that sounds exactly like a 1970s rock song but sung in a fake southern accent. In the spirit of inclusiveness, we've added the following categories: Best one-legged singer; best singer who never quite went pro and had to keep a day job; and best singer to have struggled with addiction and the loss of a grandparent, was bullied in school, and is dyslexic. At the end of the night, stick around for the big country-opera jam!

Ballet: In the world of ballet, there would be awards for best pirouette, best leap, best man carrying woman overhead, tightest buns, best leotards, cutest tights, most delightful tutu, and best man walking around the stage like he's trying to keep from pooping in his pants.

Why can't people just be who they are and not compare themselves to anyone else? Why create competitions? I would bet that it was first done to sell something: Test your skill and strength! Come to town square at 3 p.m. on Saturday to see who can roll the stone wheel the fastest! The winner receives 10,000 shekels! Entry fee is only 300 shekels! Only 100 shekels to sit and watch (and buy a pint or two of grog and a slice of yummy lamb intestines)!

I am pleading with you, my fine-feathered reader, to visit all my social media sites and follow me. Then, if you would, please click the like button on every post I've ever made and give me wonderful, raving comments. This year, I've been nominated in one category. I need your support so that I can claim in my advertising that I'm the best at adamantly, firmly, loudly telling my wife that I absolutely, *most assuredly did* put the car keys back in the top drawer left of the kitchen sink, then come to find out that I actually *hadn't* put them there after she found them in the pants pocket of a pair of my jeans at the bottom of the clothes hamper.

SCAM ARTIST

Hello. I'm here today at the city dump, sifting through all of this sweet rubbish, looking for pieces of credit cards that people have cut up before throwing them in the waste bin. I also keep a keen eye peeled for those long strips of paper from a shredder as I forage on my hands and knees. I hated it when new shredders appeared on the market that cut the paper into bits instead of the long strips. Darn it! It was easy to tape the strips back together and recreate a savings account number to steal from. Not so easy to deal with the bits.

 I'll take all the credit card scraps that I find here, then drive my old pile-of-crap clunker car back home to my hot-as-hell trailer in a mobile home park called I'll Be Damned If I Ever Pull Weeds Again Mobile Village, where every square inch of the ten-acre facility is covered in pavement, concrete, or gravel.

 I'll enter my sweet champion-hoarder-of-all-time mobile domicile and sit in my filthy, incredibly cluttered office. Next, I'll put on my dirty, scratched reading magnifiers and try to splice together the bits of cut-up credit cards and paper scraps to make a full account number, or any kind of information that I can use to divert funds into my own funnel. I will then laugh maniacally, with a tint of evil, as I imagine the shock and horror on people's pitiful faces when they find out I've bilked their credit card company and charged hundreds (sometimes more than a thousand) dollars on the card number I pieced together from my dump findings.

Knowing all this, would you believe that I don't consider myself a bad person? A sniveling, whiny, namby-pamby, milksop, finagler, yes. Bad person? No. I believe society at large owes me the kind of life that I had planned for myself but was not able to achieve. Do you ever feel that way?

I was actively working toward being a productive member of society. I had decided to be a professional freestyle Dining Room Table Refinishing While Skydiving athlete. I tried and tried for eight years in a row but never finished higher than twelfth in the national standings. I barely eked out a living but was hopeful I would soon start winning competitions, climbing the ladder of success, and thereby improving my standard of living. One income stream for these athletes was royalties from appearing on TV during a competition. The more screen time, the more pay. The better-looking participants got the tiger's share of the royalties. I wasn't too happy with that. I felt I wasn't unattractive but figured I had better start finishing higher rather than rest on my fading looks.

One day, with no warning, I was forced to take a drug test. The results showed I had high levels of anabolic steer hemorrhoids in my blood. The board of directors of the Dining Room Table Refinishing While Skydiving Association kicked me out for cheating, but everyone was doing it! I believe I was singled out for the random test because I was older than all the other athletes and I was not considered good-looking anymore. They wanted to recruit younger, prettier people. (I was once a very pretty person. I was. I *was*. I WAS!)

After being banned from my chosen sport, I got even by turning to a life of addiction and scamming. Why not? The sport of freestyle Dining Room Table Refinishing While Skydiving had turned its back on me. What was I supposed to do, become a french-fry flipper? I made one last attempt at succeeding in an above-board pursuit before I slid into a world of unrestrained substance misuse and hoodwinking.

I tried to make a go of rock music, where I felt I could dominate the industry. I chose a four-string bass guitar as my weapon, with which I would spring forth and become a household name across North America and the world. It seemed that it would be easy to quickly master the instrument and the music. I figured a fast track to fame would be to attend a rock-and-roll fantasy camp. I'd learn from the best, then hit the ground running, right?

Five of my favorite bass players—Michael Anthony, Ida Neilsen, Tony Franklin, Esperanza Spalding, and Matt Bissonette—were my instructors. Wow! They were all fun, friendly, and patient as I struggled to comprehend and play the bass line from Van Halen's "Running with the Devil." My fingers were trembling. I was sweating and red-faced from constantly making mistakes. Matt offered me a gem of advice: "Hey, man, just play for an audience of one. It's just you and your higher power." I loved that advice, but as a soon-to-be scam artist, I didn't have a higher power. I was a self-centered, empty shell of a human. Maybe Matt's advice will someday creep into my consciousness and allow me to evolve, but for now I was staying focused on achieving the massive fame and fortune that was owed to me.

After an entire day at the Rock 'n' Roll Fantasy Camp with Michael, Ida, Tony, Esperanza, and Matt cheering me on, giving me one-on-one instruction and revealing guarded, inside tips and tricks, I just couldn't get it. I wasn't musically skilled enough to play the piece. I left the camp defeated and dejected, with my goal deflected. Michael Anthony was very kind and gave me a three-pack of his famous Mad Anthony's Hot Sauce as a consolation. I walked out to my old pile-of-crap clunker, drove slowly back to my hot-as-hell champion-hoarder-of-all-time mobile home, and plopped down at my desk to reassess my life's purpose and think of something to do.

One day I Googled *Do I need to be addicted to a substance in order to become a highly successful person?* According to the search results, the answer was yes. Nearly all successful people had a secret (or not-so-secret) fixation with and overindulgence of a substance or activity, such as food, alcohol, drugs, ski passes at the best mountain resorts, boats, or kinky sexual practices. Since I didn't have any real money at the time, I chose to acquire an overuse of an affordable substance.

Next, I did a search for *I need a new addiction and method of income.* Up popped several bookstore websites, all of which offered a book that was serendipitously titled *100 Fun New Addictions.* Feeling lucky, I suddenly felt that things might soon be going my way. I ordered the book and waited in my dark, unbelievably untidy and smelly home. (The stench was from years of cooking horrid, unpalatable meals of various foul meats. I can't remember who was president the last time I opened the windows or cleaned the stovetop or oven. Grease dripped from the kitchen ceiling, and the odor was permanently embedded in my hair, clothing, carpet, drapes, and walls.)

Finally, after two agonizingly long days, the book arrived at my front door. I dove in, eyes first, and began scanning the contents. It was chuck full of great addiction ideas. (What did you say? The term is *chock* full? That's just stupid. No. It's *chuck* full. Yes it is! The term originated from a guy named Chuck, who counted all the cats and dogs that fell through a thatched roof when it was raining really hard one day, okay? Let's just drop it and move on!)

I started trying the ideas in the book right away, progressing from one to the next. I broke into houses to smell other people's unwashed pillowcases. That thrill became a bore after six weeks. The next suggested fixation became drinking grapefruit-scented hand lotion. Soon I had moved on to cramming peanuts in my ear canals.

The worst obsession was the most expensive and, thankfully, the last. At an industrial hardware supply store where I had run up a huge credit debt, one kindly old saleswoman recognized that something wasn't right with me. One day, while I was purchasing eight boxes of zinc-plated socket-head M10 x 1.5 x 101.6 mm-long bolts, she noticed the drool running out of the corner of my mouth because the Novocain hadn't worn off yet from a dental procedure I'd had earlier that day. She wrote something on a piece of paper and slid it across the counter to me. I pretended I didn't understand what she had written, but took the note with me.

I joined a therapy support group. Every Thursday evening at seven o'clock I went to the local community center building in room 243 and participated in the chanting-and-sharing session for Why Am I Addicted to Eating Metric Bolts? It was a welcome relief to get rid of the constant lust for bolts and the related costly dental work.

I devoted more time to and got creative with my scamming to bring in more greenbacks. I was building up an arsenal of techniques using email and phone calls, but I wanted a new obsession that would fuel my drive to wildly succeed at my flimflamming.

I acquired a co-swindler in India. We sold each other phone number lists. I called people in India and, speaking in Hindi with an American accent, tried to convince them to buy an extended car warranty. He called people in America and, speaking in English with a Hindi accent, told them that the IRS has found mistakes and needed their social security number.

At the same time, I was lonely and felt it was time to have a loving partner. I knew I would never be able to attract my ideal life partner unless I had ducats spilling out of my pockets. I craved a superficial woman who wanted me for my material offerings. I had tried attending a yoga retreat in order to find a mate, but I misread the flier that was stapled to the print-and-copy shop bulletin board. It was actually a yogurt retreat. I left that event just as defeated and embarrassed as I had felt after my rock-and-roll fantasy camp experience.

I placed a personal ad in my local town newspaper: *Looking for a life partner. You don't have to be height-weight proportionate. Can be any race or gender identification. Please be over 42 years old. Must be unpredictable and argumentative. Move to the head of the line if you have unhealthy food obsessions, are severely jealous, and have one or more estranged and troublesome children between the ages of 18 and 56.*

I rarely left my sweet, stenchy hoarder's paradise to venture into my local town, so it was not likely I would have a chance meeting with a compatible counterpart. I had profiles on many dating sites, like Scamming Singles, Romantic Rip-offs, and Deceitful Darlings, hoping that I would find that elusive mate because I was online-dating sixteen different women. Every one of them told me I was the best man they had ever encountered online.

I was still attending my metric-bolt-eating therapy group. One evening we were introduced to a method whereby one replaces a current addiction with another that is intended to be less damaging and costly than the first. Have you heard of bubble-wrap-popping therapy? This is where the addict pops the bubbles in bubble wrap.

I loved it. (Doesn't it feel good to pop those suckers?) At first I did it with my fingers, then moved on to biting them. Then I progressed to walking barefoot on sheets of those irresistible little plastic globules of air. I got so obsessed with doing it that I forgot all about eating metric bolts. Yay! Right?

Well, kind of. My dental bills dropped way off, but I was ordering and popping a thousand dollars-a-month's worth of bubble wrap! I was sneaking it every chance I got, doing it in closets and bathrooms. I found a bubble-popping-fanatics group online. We eventually got tired of having Zoom and Skype popping sessions and began to meet in person.

I knew it had gotten out of hand when I found myself with five women, three men, a chicken, and a bag of talcum powder. One day, we were all wearing nothing but bright red wigs and Ronald Reagan masks in a motel room at the Quality Inn on Lanier Avenue in Fayetteville, Georgia (including the chicken). After four hours of rolling around naked on sheet after sheet of bubble wrap, pop-pop-popping the night away while Michael Bublé's songs wafted from the Apple Music app on my phone, I stood up and candidly announced I was done with being a bubble popper and would be moving on to breaking-glass therapy. "Who wants to join me?" I asked. Only the chicken was game.

BUY MY BOOK

I used to be a crastinator, and although I was quite good, I was still an amateur. With practice, however, I got better at it and was able to allow any and all distractions to sidestep my writing; that's when I achieved the level of pro-crastinator.

I needed to write my second book. My regular hairstylist at Buzz That Mop told me that the best way to have people discover my first book is to put out another one. Often, in the related artistic field of music, bands and musicians don't get discovered with their introductory release. For example, the skeptical rock countryside is littered with inaugural songs and albums that didn't fully connect with audiences. At some point, people discovered an artist's latest release and, having become fans, unearthed earlier offerings.

I was advised that it's the same in the book world. An author must go through the process of creating a first book to get experience and find out what people like or don't like. The wise scribe who is paying attention will build upon that information to further develop a unique style. Hopefully, then, the second book will turn out better and pull in a larger audience that is curious to find out what else the author has done.

If you're curious to know what else I've done, here are three things:

1. When I was in the US Air Force, I grew alfalfa sprouts and made yogurt in my dorm room.
2. The first time I had intimate relations was in the backseat of a 1972 Oldsmobile Toronado.
3. I was caught stealing a Hot Wheels car at Toy and Patio Village in Sierra Madre, California, when I was seven years old.

Now back to the concept of artists continuing to put out new material in the hopes that people will discover their earlier output. There is one example that is so fantastic that I must tell it here. The great writer Kurt Vonnegut had five books published over a twelve-year span but was still relatively unknown; all five books were out of print by 1967. In 1969, seventeen years after his first novel was published, *Slaughterhouse-Five* was released and rocketed Vonnegut to fame. His publishing house cleverly and wisely repackaged all five previously released books and put them back into print. They also roared up the charts.

In my case, if it takes seventeen years between my first published book and my rocket ride to literary stardom, fine. I'll be seventy-eight. I should be in good enough shape to still swim laps in the motorcycle-shaped pool that I'll have installed in my backyard. I'll drive dangerously fast in one of my Lamborfarri sports cars and, on a whim, fly to London in my Lear jet to see the latest Elton John concert. He'll be ninety-two and in the seventeenth year of his Farewell Tour.

I certainly don't claim to be in Vonnegut's league, but I must brag and say that my first book firmly established me as a powerhouse player in the "I'm No Longer a Wannabe Writer Because I Wrote My First Book as a Middle-Aged Person" competition. (This *is* a competition, right?)

Have you noticed that people who are actually in the "old" category push the boundary of middle age higher and higher as they themselves get older? At sixty-two, I consider myself a youthful middle-aged person; I still laugh at the sound of my own farts.

At the time of this writing in September 2022, the average person's life expectancy is seventy-nine years. Middle age, then, would be a ten-year bracket of thirty-four and a half to forty-four and a half years. That's crazy and ridiculous. If the middle of seventy-nine years is thirty-nine and a half years, sixty-two would technically be old. But I'm not old! I'm not. I'm *not!* And what about those who lived during the Middle Ages? Life expectancy was only thirty-three years. One could say that middle age during the Middle Ages was sixteen and a half years! That's mind-boggling now, isn't it? Rock stars who didn't die at twenty-seven would live only six more years!

Since I'm fond of this ponder, I'll carry onward. Is it

okay to call myself a writer at the moderately advanced age of sixty-two? To *write* that I'm a writer? To say *out loud* that I'm a writer? When people ask me what I do, I still timidly reply, "I'm a heating and air conditioning professional, a songwriter, a lyricist, a bass guitarist, a vocalist, a generally nice person, a motorcycle enthusiast, a problem solver, and a writer." I need to start proudly proclaiming (instead of amateur-claiming) my true calling. Going forward, when I fill out loan applications and forms at the doctor's office, I will write *Freakin' Writer* in the blank space where they ask for my occupation.

In that regard, now that I'm trying to become a bona fide scribe, I've decided to start smoking a pipe, and I'll soon change my name to Douglas Henry Margaret Fergus. Better yet, I'll use initials for my first names, DHM Fergus.

There is another issue that affects the creative output and drive of an artist: struggle. Oodles of artists lived through awful relationships with parents, grandparents, siblings, and spouses. Gobs of famous woodcarvers, oil painters, and fantasy novel authors have revealed in their autobiographies that these aforementioned strifes are what pushed them to achieve, to prove *them* wrong, to *get even*. Gosh darn it, I think I'll have to bring a lawsuit against all my family members. I had a nice, uneventful upbringing.

To be more like a real true author, should I scrawl in cursive under candlelight on a legal tablet? What about using a hammer and chisel on a stone tablet? Should I swallow tablets while doing it? Shall I jot down witticisms using a feather pen and India ink? How about wearing a fifteenth-century period-correct outfit, including a long-sleeved shirt with frilly cuffs? Maybe not, because when I tried that, the cuffs were always getting ink on them and then I'd drag them across the page and leave black smears.

    I bet my author status would improve as a cigarette smoker. Isn't that what real writers do? I could sit writing in an outdoor café in, say, London. I would let the cancer stick dangle rakishly from my lips while the rising smoke burned my eyes. I would let the ash portion get precariously long, then I'd get upset when it fell on the keys of my laptop computer. I would startle the other café customers by pounding on the table and blurting, "Oh, shunder puff!" I would take long, slow drags, then exhale while speaking with a slight mumble as I greeted anyone who passed by my table. I would start every sentence with, "You see..." In publicity interviews, I would answer questions with non sequiturs, saying things like, "You see, I like chocolate when rainy days and mushroom pillows subsist on mediocrity inside the white candle placemats of squeaky tantamount gallery porridge."

    I've read that many famous writers drank alcoholic beverages to excess late at night and loitered about with eccentric people. They would have spirited discussions about shallow sea fishing, Italian operas prior to 1632, wax-resistant fabric dyeing techniques, and clay pigeon shooting.

    I think it might behoove me to gather a circle of friends who are much younger than me. I could then feel fatherly (grandfatherly?) and impress them with facts and fabrications about my life from before they were born. "I remember when gasoline was twenty-five cents per gallon and a candy bar could be had for ten cents!" One young, gorgeous brunette person would exclaim, "Oh, wow! That's totally amazing! You've lived a very long time, haven't you?!" I could gather a gaggle of youngsters who would call me Boss or Gramps or simply Dougie. I would have a huge, unkempt gray beard, but my long, greasy hair would be kempt.

I would throw lavish, outrageous parties in my one-bedroom apartment, financed with my credit card. All the attendees would talk among themselves that I was a mildly fascinating, sad, desperate character who was still craving fame at an age when most people are in a state of reclination. I would get wind of the youthful guests snickering behind my back and feel weirdly satisfied that being a mildly fascinating, sad, desperate character would make me an even *more* interesting person and a better writer.

I would do shirtless belly flops into the awkwardly small apartment complex pool, splashing water onto the shoes, pant bottoms, and legs of the guests standing along the edge. The men would chuckle in amusement, wishing their fathers could be more like me.

The bacchanalian bashes (wild gatherings involving excessive drinking and physical pleasuring) thrown by my youthful friends would end at three, four, or sometimes five in the morning. All the attendees would flee to their respective love nests, and I would be left alone to lie, contented but forlorn, in my bed, holding my phone and scrolling endlessly through Brag-o-gram. I would get drunk on envy looking at tantalizing posts from the smartest, most inspiring people on the planet showing what they ate for dinner, exercising their firm buttocks and biceps, and relentlessly wallowing in the nostalgia of events in their careers from thirty, forty, and even fifty years before.

In order to maximize my creative output, should I move to New York City? How about Paris, France? Or better yet, Perris, California? Would my writing career zoom forth if I moved to delightful Detroit, Michigan; heavenly Hemet, California; or the safe, serene, nifty and neato Naples, Italy?

To afford my rent without the income and burden of a day job, I would place an ad for roommates so they could help pay. They would all be idiosyncratic, slovenly, and noisy, and would, curiously, always occupy the bathroom just when I needed to use it, adding more character-building stress to my life that I could recount later in a novel, play, or movie. I would call this future blockbuster *Lease*. What's that you say? The idea has been taken! You're telling me that there is already a hugely successful Broadway play called *Rent*? Gosh dang it!

(Hello, dear reader. Did you intend to open and read this book? If so, thank you. You can safely disregard this message. If you did *not* intend to open this book, please immediately call our security hotline at 1-800-BIGDUMMY.)

* * *

My second book was taking shape, coming together like a finely prepared gourmet meal or the punctilious restoration of an exquisite, rare, coveted 1967 Bultaco Metralla motorcycle.

Anticipating the enormous royalty stream about to begin after my second book was published, I was giddy with glee. (Isn't Giddy Glee the bassist and vocalist in the rock band Rush?) I had self-published my first book and was riding high on the reviews and royalties that were dribbling in. I was able to afford a really fancy coffee drink at Starstrucks once a week!

Wait. On second thought, I wouldn't *become* a writer, I would shed my previous life and simply *be* a writer. My very core would ooze punctuation, verbs, nouns, and objectives. (What's that you say? Oh.) I'm told the word is *adjectives*. Okay. You don't need to dangle a participle in front of me to lead me to my typewriter.

Writing would choose me, the same way that baseball chose Babe Ruth, motion pictures chose Meryl Streep, and the Seat Cushion Seamstresses League of America chose Phyllis H. Grumbleclop to spend thirty-five continual years stuffing blocks of foam rubber into floral-print recreational vehicle seat covers. (She never got promoted to the sewing shut of seat cushions, but she remained a cheerful worker through nine United States presidential administrations. "I never wanted the freakin' stress," she quipped to the local newspaper reporter who asked at her retirement party why she never graduated to seamstress.)

Since I'm vacillating like an oscillating fan, I will ask you: Once I hit the big time, should I buy a boat? I believe the best writers have boats, don't they? I suppose I don't even need to use it, considering I can't swim and I get severely motion sick just from sitting in a rocking chair. What should I name it? Misty Morning Typewriter? Grammatical Errors? No, I believe it needs to be something about laziness or drinking alcohol to be a legitimate name. I think my best choice would be a sailboat. There is no motor to deal with, and all the rope-tying and sail-hoisting that is required might make me seem more ruggedly manly. That may expand my reader base by appealing to book buyers who like rugged and manly men.

I could move to a sweet, sleepy coastal town and find an affordable little port, a place like Yas Marina in Abu Dhabi, United Arab Emirates. Instead of buying a boat, I would rent one to see if I liked the writer-and-boater lifestyle. I would stop shaving my facial hair and become a scraggly, randomly grumpy, aloof character. I would wear the same old blue-and-white checkered deck sneakers with tan slacks and a blue button-down, short-sleeved shirt every day. I'd wear a faux sea captain's hat, and whenever I did speak to people, I'd call them Captain. Even if they obviously had never and would never go fishing ever in their lives, I'd start the conversation with, "How's the fishing today, Captain?" Then I'd end with, "Fish on, Captain."

※ ※ ※

After a trillion hours of cogitation, meditation, and deliberation, I settled on moving to a different country, hanging out in coffee houses and bars, and trying to speak to the locals in their language. I was thrilled to journey to a new country and establish an artistic residency.

In the months after my relocation to Turnupisia, I stumbled through superficial conversations with locals, never getting beyond, "How are you? What is your favorite color? I also like Formica countertops." I arranged interviews with the local press and radio, stating, "I live in Turnupisia full-time now. I'm too cool to live in America. Isn't that where *Americans* live? Ugh."

I was wild with delight upon discovering that my neighbors were the fabulous writer David Sedaris and his partner, Hugh. We lived in a sixteenth-century six-story apartment building. David and Hugh resided on the sixth floor in a spacious, gorgeous suite lavishly decorated with stunning art objects of marble and carbon-bran, skillfully created by the finest Italian craftspeople in the style of the glorious Benadryl period. Their humongous windows revealed views of the luscious Paprika-upon-Thyme River. When guests visited, they were required to reach into a box, find their size, and put on ergonomically shaped clogs, carved out of rare Brazilian Ooga-Chalka wood with pieces of Siberian goat felt from the ancient city of Lagash glued to the bottoms of the soles to make walking a quiet and non-slip affair.

The ravishing grounds (name for a coffee shop!) surrounding the property were expertly and meticulously maintained on a daily basis by a team of youthful, attractive, sprightly, tight-coveralls-wearing Turnupisian women and men. There was no need, in truth, for me or David to have a lawnmower, but I bought one anyway. He and Hugh had a huge overhanging AstroTurf-covered deck. Just for fun, once a week during the summer grass-growing season, I carried the grass-cutting machine up the six flights of stairs (no elevators in our ancient building), then pushed it back and forth across their deck, pretending to shorten the fescues. I hoped that David would find me idiosyncratic and write about me in one of his future books.

My ground-floor apartment, on the other hand, was a small, cramped, damp, accessible-by-ramp studio flat painted with that lovely Benjamin More, More, Moore catalog color #24, Inside of Bovine Belly. All the shelves, chairs, couches, and tables were built by yours truly. I gathered (stole) several rough, splintered, greasy pallets that I got from behind Brunella's Boat and Bus Crankshafts, LLC. I stacked and nailed them together to make alluring, beguiling, and functionally awkward furniture that all my roommates and guests rave about. When David and Hugh dropped in for a stainless-steel camping cup of gooseberry wine, they both requested to sit on my pallet sofa!

They were super-duper nice. I mean that in the superest, duperest way. (Is it a sign of the decline of humanity that my autocorrect program is not trying to correct *superest* or *duperest?*) Our conversations were the deepest. Both of them were fascinating guests. We chatted about worldly subjects like motorcycles, cars, trucks, guitars, bodybuilding, and the odd, enchanting

Turnupisian heating systems. I shied away from discussing subjects such as politics, religion, organic farming, twelfth-century playwrights, vegan cheesemaking, and nonflammable roofing materials. I didn't want them to feel intimidated.

*　*　*

Doesn't anybody read anymore? Seriously. Doesn't anybody ever turn a page?

I'm scratching out my next manuscript with a nail on a piece of tar paper. Surrounding me are my only friends, the rafters. Gosh dang, it's hot up here in this attic. My household is too noisy and chaotic for me to be able to focus and write, so I squeeze up the narrow, steep steps to the serene, stuffy, stifling stillness that the fiberglass-insulated workspace offers.

In case you're wondering, *Why is he writing about an attic? Do first-floor apartments have attics?* Well, um, I ran out of money and had to leave Turnupisia. I bid a tearful adieu to my wonderful apartment neighbors, David and Hugh. They were nice enough to buy all my handmade furniture for a fair price, which covered my airfare back to America.

I found an inexpensive, sweet little house to rent in lovely and safe Bessemer, Alabama. I shared it with a wonderful family of four, but as I said, I needed a quiet place to create. The attic is dusty, dirty, always hot (no matter what time of year), and there are many scraps of old shingles and tar paper strewn about from the last time the roof was boisterously replaced by a crew of friendly, happy, recovering, galumphing, profanity-spewing workers. Did I mention it's darn hot up here? Hey! That's a great opening line! I'll write it down so I don't forget it. *Did I mention it's darn hot up here?* Oh, no, no, no! That's a crappy line. Forget it.

(Decades ago, I would rip the paper out of the typewriter, crinkle it up, and toss it into the nearest waste bin. If you're old enough to have used an actual typewriter, did you do the same when you got frustrated at making too many mistakes? Or did you *crumple* up the paper? To crinkle or crumple, that is the question. There are two types of people in the world: crinklers and crumplers. Tonight, appearing on the main stage at the comedy festival, It's Crinkle and Crumple!)

Anyway, I thought life would change when the reflection of my brain (i.e., my first book) was put into a box and wrapped with cellophane. I gave mirror speeches and practiced signing my name. But bookstore customers only look, flip the pages, and put it back on the shelf. Won't you please buy my book?

One fine day I was cruising toward town, riding on the city bus. I was lost in a daydream fantasy. I like to pretend that I'm easily recognized. Do you do that too? It would be fun to be a star for a day or two. Maybe just long enough to get the Rolls Royce and a book-shaped pool. Then I'd contact StarForADaydotcom and tell them to turn off my celebrity status (until I needed another ego boost), but I'd want to keep the Rolls and the pool. I yelled at the bus driver, *"Pare en la nombre de amor!"* (Stop in the name of love!) at the intersection of Disenchantment

Avenue and Heartbreak Boulevard. I stepped off, walked to a still-functioning pay phone, and called my manager. He didn't recognize my name or voice. Crud! Do I or don't I have an agent? Oh, foo-fa-roonie anyway.

I walked along the streets of Laredo to my post office box. No fan letters or royalty checks (sad face emoji). Foo-fa-roonie! Next, I dropped in at my local bookstore. I put on sunglasses so they wouldn't recognize me. I had planned to buy another copy of my own book. (I do that to prove to the bookstore owner that my book is popular and she needs to order more copies.) I walked to aisle 34 and pretended to look for my title. I knew it was in the humor section, third row from the bottom, four feet from the right end cap. I located it and took one out. "We want only two copies for now," the owner had said while discussing consignment terms. "We'll see how well it sells and adjust inventory later."

I casually leaned against a shelf and shifted my hip to one side, indicating I was a relaxed browser. I opened the book, started turning the pages, and got a flash of disbelief. Oh foo-fa-roonie! Can it be?! The entire chapter three was missing! I took out the other copy, and sure enough, both copies were missing chapter three. I didn't want to cause a scene, so I kept my cool, put both books back, and quietly slinked out of the store.

Oh, these devious vanity book publishers! I suppose they have to keep their overhead low, but come on! Leaving out my precious chapter three? Sheesh-a-Marie!

✶ ✶ ✶

After my self-published first book had been out for a year, I decided to hire a book promotions company to help with marketing to get more sales. I was a single man when I walked into the office of Gargantuan Lollipop Publishing. I didn't have the levelheaded skepticism of a partner, mother, brother, or anyone named Carruthers or Struthers to balance out my uncontrollable urge for instant gratification. The sweet-talking sales reps (all gorgeous, honey-voiced women) convinced me to fork over a truckload of bucks for their Platinum Plan. I fell top-over-toes with them and enthusiastically shared my account and routing numbers so they could pull moola from my bank whenever they desired. When my bank balance had been exhausted, they arranged a convenient high-interest loan to cover the remainder of the fees. I was thoroughly convinced that the $24,599.00 for them to re-proofread, re-edit, re-typeset, and completely change the cover art was a bargain. And gosh, the low minimum order of only forty thousand copies at my wholesale cost of $14.95 each was a deal!

At first, the marketing plan that Gargantuan Lollipop developed for me showed promise. I understood that they were too busy to actually carry out the plan themselves, that I was paying them for the brainwork to develop a strategy. Soon the sales began to seep in. A distant cousin whom I hadn't communicated with since Ronald Reagan was president bought a copy. A high school friend I hadn't spoken to in thirty-five years purchased one after my one o'clock a.m. buzzed-on-rum-and-diet-Dr.-Pepper phone call woke him up. "Hi, Rick! I found your profile on Facebook, then paid $99.95 for a pro-level people search to get your phone number! How have you been?!" He wasn't happy, especially considering that the last time I had spoken to him, "My Sharona" was the number one song of the year, and we were having a Mr. Pibb guzzling contest with Billy Freemteagan in the far back booth of Loueddie's Pizza in Lake Arrowhead. "Will you leave me alone if I promise to order a copy on Amazon?" he sleepily grumbled into the phone, not hiding his perturbance.

My favorite local supermarket checker took a copy and promised to compensate me on her next payday. One of my apartment building neighbors stuck a check under my car windshield wiper after a midnight scamper, when I had leaned a book against each of the seven front doors to the right of my house and the seven to the left, then scurried back to my residence. I withdrew the paper remittance from between the wiper and glass and found it was for five dollars, not the $14.95 price printed on the book. A year later, at a neighborhood block party, I finally got the courage to ask if anyone knew who had left me the check for five dollars. "Oh, that was me," replied an older woman whom I recognized from seeing her out walking with three dogs every morning. She casually said, "I felt that was all it was worth to me."

Regarding the other thirteen books I had left against the nearby residents' doors, seven of them remained lying haphazardly on their respective welcome mats for months, having been ignored, kicked, stepped on, and treated as stray trash. I assume that the remaining six were taken in, but I never heard a word and never received any compensation from those home dwellers.

One day I tried standing in front of the supermarket with a cardboard box on which I had written FREE KITTENS. When people stepped up, delighted at the prospect of viewing the darling little creatures, I blurted out, "Only kidding! Wouldn't you rather have one of my books?" I sold only one paperback, to a sweet little old lady who handed over a ten-spot, then promptly took the book and hit me upside the head with it. I was being sarcastic when I wrote that the marketing plan I had developed showed promise. It was a lousy plan. A no-plan plan. A wop-bop a-loo-bop a-lop bad plan.

While I wallowed in the mire of my desire to earn a National Medal of Arts in literature from some future president, I decided to attend a seminar, Learn How to Write Commercial Crap that Half-a-Brains Will Buy. It was at this event, in the lobby between the vegan cupcakes vending machine and the entrance to the janitor closet, that I met my mate.

What started out as a casual interest has become the one sure thing. She is the enchanting and captivating Folio Flipper. Yep, that's her real given name. We bonded on day two of the workshop, Clothing Optional Day. Out of forty-eight attendees, we were the only two who chickened out and remained attired. Following the seminar, we had a tepid, dawdling, three-month courtship that cemented our geek union. One day I asked Folio, "Um, do you, I mean, would you wanna, um, like, start, like, being a couple?" With incisive ambivalence, she muttered, "I guess." We were both overcome with vacillating certainty that we were perfect for each other.

Three months after we met, we were living happily together and had two pet turtles, Flo and Eddie. I knew I needed to reveal my paid marketing blunder and that I was not smart enough to navigate by myself the intricacies of the sneaky co-marketing agreement I had signed with Gargantuan Lollipop Publishing. Sweet Folio guided me through the process of legally extricating myself from the contract. It took three years, two lawyers, and a large advance on Folio's inheritance from her grandmother's fortune.

(Folio's grandmother, Leaflet Flipper, had created that 1970s craze Pump Yarn and Perspire! It was an exercise program that was advertised on late-night TV for gullible couch potatoes. For only $19.99 you would receive a kit that included knitting needles, a big ball of yarn, a soft foam rubber mat, and a booklet with various exercises to be performed while knitting and listening to music. Also inside the box was a cassette containing danceable re-recordings of hits of the day, but with new lyrics to suit the knitting theme: "I Want You to Knit Me a Hat," by Peter Frampton; "More than a Sweater," by the Bee Gees; "Tie a Yellow Scarf 'round the Old Oak Tree," by Tony Orlando and Dawn. The craze got so popular that Leaflet sold the manufacturing and distribution rights but kept 10 percent of the future profits. At the height of the craze, 426 million units had been sold, but the timing was perfect for her to let go of the operation. Soon after, the craze petered out, and the company that had acquired Pump Yarn and Perspire, LLC went bankrupt.)

* * *

I really tested Folio's patience because of my ignorance of financial matters. I don't blame her at all for losing confidence that I could manage my life as an adult. What a dipstick I was! I thank the universal goddesses and gods every day for sending Folio to me. I promised her that I would never again get entangled in a contract without consulting her first. My big boo-boo was assuming I would sell at least enough books to break even. But why was that a mistake? Why shouldn't I expect to at least break even? What's wrong with the general public? What's wrong with the universe? Doesn't anybody read anymore? Doesn't anyone ever turn a page?

Folio told me that she had written a book several years ago. It was an exercise method for snails called *From the Garden to the Treadmill: A Life Avoiding Salt*. She had carefully chosen a legitimate vanity publishing company to handle the printing, then tried her best to market and promote the copies everywhere she could. She sold them at every stop whenever she drove her car but had a problem with paper dust and shredded pages coming out from the engine compartment. She admitted sheepishly, "I finally figured out that I had been selling copies of my book out of the *hood* of my car instead of the *trunk*. The books were getting caught up in the radiator fan."

"OMG, Folio!" I blurted. "You're a funny bunny!"

"Also," she continued with mock glumness, "I had been banking on the royalties streaming in. I was sure I'd be awash in royalties. I was hoping to be floating on a river of royalties." I said, "If you can come up with one more royalty-slash-water analogy, I'll take you to lunch."

"Okay." She smiled. "I dreamed of the day I would dogpaddle around in a pool underneath a waterfall of royalties."

"Wow, three water references in one analogy. I'll buy you three lunches!" I replied.

Folio then told me she got a review of her book that was obviously a sign from Gosh. "Folio Flipper is a walnut brain. Her pedestrian scribbling left me screaming in agony, convulsing on the proverbial literary crosswalk of life."

"After that review, I had to take a long, intrinsic, inherent look at my yearning to be a writer," she intoned. "I asked myself, *who am I trying to impress?*"

I said, "Or is it *whom* am I trying to impress? I can never remember when to do that. I think the rule is: I before E except after whom."

Folio didn't acknowledge my attempt at humor and continued. "Was I trying to prove someone wrong? A parent, teacher, former boss, or playground bully? Did I need to die at twenty-seven years old to immortalize myself and ensure that my next of kin would receive my royalties for decades after my passing? Do authors die at twenty-seven, or only rock musicians?" (For you rock musicians twenty-eight or older, did you breathe a sigh of relief on your twenty-eighth birthday? Phew! Made it!)

Folio advised me that in order to achieve one's goals, one cannot do it from a place of comfort. "You can't do it from a place of ease and deep, soft cushions. A lush, plush chaise lounge in a grandiose home may prevent you from achieving your goal. You must work from a place of discomfort, which is what drives you to achieve. Even after you become successful, you don't want to fall into the trap of surrounding yourself with delicacies, elegance, and refinements that are conducive to sumptuous living."

I took that advice to heart. That is why I am writing this book now, sitting on a creaky, wobbly, filthy, splintered wooden box. My laptop computer rests upon a wooden table that was used for slaughtering hedgehogs and hasn't been cleaned since Harvey's Happy Hedgehog Processing Plant closed in 1974. Above me hangs a single dim, dusty lightbulb, and I play an old cassette recording of my fifth-grade teacher yelling at me to hurry up and finish my math assignment.

Here's an idea: You know how pop-song lyrics repeat over and over to drum the words into our heads and make us remember them? What about doing that with books? I'll be the first author to do it. I'll write a short story of about twenty pages and then just repeat the same story until the book is two hundred fifty pages long! No? Okay, at least I'm thinking and trying, right?

Then I thought I might try being a serious writer. In my publicity photos, I'd never smile. That way, I'd remain mysterious and readers would go berserk trying to find out what I was *really* like in person. Speaking of serious writers, there's nothing funny about peace, love, and the romance genre. Do you agree that there aren't enough romance books on the planet? Statistics show that there is only one romance author for every person alive on Earth. That's not enough! Then again, what if I become a murder mystery writer? Can there be too many of those? On the other hand, we certainly don't have enough psychological-slash-military-slash-thriller books.

In any case, I have to hurry and crank out a bunch of books while I'm still here on the planet. I want my biography to be bursting with accolades, boasting that I'm an award-winning author of thirty-eight novels, nine books of short stories, and eleven screenplays. But here I am at sixty-two years young, pitifully working on only my second book.

I've been dreaming of using a small portion of my future enormous monthly royalty checks to buy a thousand-acre winery property in Sonoma County, just like the famous writer Jack London. I'll have the rows of grapes planted in such a way as to be in the shape of a typewriter when viewed from an airplane. How about a typewriter-shaped pool? I think we can all agree it would be fun to have a swimming pool in the shape of one of our favorite things. How about a pool in the shape of a creepy, old, abandoned shopping mall? The Rolling Acres mall in Akron, Ohio, would fit the bill nicely. Abandoned since 2013, its shape would make a perfect family water recreation feature.

Speaking of pools in the shape of our favorite things, I'm a big fan of bundling. You too? I'm talking *packs* of things. I typically don't want just one of anything. Some of my most cherished items come in packs. I'd want a pool in the shape of a six-pack of malt liquor, an eight-pack of blueberry-muffin-flavored Kit Kat candy bars, or a ten-pack of 300-count Q-Tip cotton swabs. How about a pool in the shape of David Pack, the singer and songwriter from the soft rock group Ambrosia?

Here's another gimmick that might make me known to the world: I could try being a big-words writer. I'd create stories where the reader would have to keep a dictionary nearby to look up complex, seldom-used words. It would be annoying to everyone except the brightest and brainiest. This perfunctory use of hefty, multisyllabic units of locution would alienate some readers, but others would be pulled in by my supposed, assumed, and implied intelligence. I would be respected ~~at the ocean boardwalk~~ by my peers. Readers would think of me as a highbrow smarty pants, but in reality I would just find giant words in a thesaurus, use them in a story, then quickly forget their meanings.

In interviews, I would have to act coy and humble. I'd pretend that I didn't know any big words so that I didn't appear pretentious and conceited. On the other foot, a different approach would be to act pretentious and conceited. Hmmm, then I would need to learn and remember the big words so I could effortlessly throw them around in interviews. I would have to be strong enough to throw them around. I would have to do word workouts. I could invent a new exercise program called Word Workouts and make tens of millions of dollars in franchise fees. My Word Workouts gyms would be located in commercial shopping centers, squeezed in between Ace Hardware stores and defunct or abandoned 1990s-era frozen yogurt shops.

Have you read about those super-famous musicians who are standoffish and rude to their fans? They feel they're superior humans because they had a great publicist, manager, and deep-pockets record company who gave radio DJs shiny new gold Cadillacs and cute little bags of "electrolytes for the nose" in exchange for massive airplay of their silly three-chord songs. The overplaying of their tunes worked their way into the public's consciousness via AM and FM radio and now play in supermarkets, airport bars, and karaoke machines.

I could try to be a conceited, condescending, pretentious prick before I become famous to see if fans flock to me. It's a given now that I'm a double threat of musician *and* writer, right? To become a coveted triple threat, I could try acting, dancing, or becoming a sewing machine repair person. Or maybe my third threat could be my incredible skill at garden maintenance. They say go for what you know, correct? In that regard, if I'm brutally honest with the self-appraisal of my true core skill set, it's an easy decision. My third threat would be cast upon the world via a new business venture. I'd hire myself out as a garden dirt-clod stomper. I doubt if any human can trample better than I can. (As a teenager, I was quite good at determining when the neighbors were not home so I could throw dirt clods over the fence into their pool.)

I've been writing "I'm a freakin' writer" two hundred times a day on a huge, six-foot by six-foot dry erase board for the last six months. I erase all of it and rewrite it every morning at three thirty. Clearly, that act alone will alert the universal goodness fairies to my desire for manifesting the life of a Pine Bluff Times (Arkansas) best-selling author.

I wonder if I'm capable of writing a colossal best-selling self-helper, like *The Celine Dion Prophecy* by James Redorchard. That would certainly set me up for life. I don't have any new or unique wit, wisdom, or meatloaf recipes to convey to a massive audience that is starving for a clear path to a better life. Then again, that never stopped other authors from writing one.

* * *

In the end, it all came down to helping others. Folio and I are still passionate writers and are always working on the next potential blockbuster, but we finally found our true calling. It was Folio's idea to develop a program where we provide authors with the tools to stay creative and keep writing every day without the encumbrance of a nine-to-five job. Folio liked my concept of hiring myself out as a dirt-clod stomper, but she envisioned others doing the stomping for me. "But Folio, dear," I asked her, "if others do the tramping, where will *my* joy come from?" She wisely replied, "Your new purpose in life is to help others find *their* bliss. In doing so, you will be rewarded with even more joy than just stomping on one clod at a time. You'll have people all over the country doing it! Imagine thousands of boots experiencing the bliss of clod stomping every day because of your selflessness in sharing your bliss!"

We now travel the country putting on seminars to teach hopeless wannabe writers—oops, I mean authors—the tools needed so they can quit their day job. All creatives are welcome to attend, but we market our course via email and social media to reach the millions who specifically dream of having a published book. If my work inspires you or simply touches you in some small way, please consider donating to your favorite charity in my name. If you don't have a favorite charity, you can always send your extra bucks to me and Folio. We are desperate for help because our dirt-clod shaped swimming pool is currently being built on our 237-acre farm in downstate New York, and a progress payment to the contractor is due.

The End

OH, YOU SILLY WORDS

I was born and raised in Southern California. Many of the streets and city names in that part of the USA were named after Hispanic places or Spanish words. In fact, the little town where I lived with my family had two Spanish words for its name: Sierra Madre. By now, in this year of our Lord and Lady of 2023, I think everyone knows that *madre* means *mother*. When we were growing up, our parents told us that *sierra* meant *mountain*. So we learned that *Sierra Madre* translated as *Mother Mountain*.

But when I was an adult and actually looked it up, the word *Sierra* (besides what hippie parents name their children and what Ford called a car that was marketed only in Europe) literally translates to *saw*, as in a device that cuts wood. I asked a Mexican friend of mine (let's call him Jose because that is his real name) and he told me that *sierra* loosely means *forested land, forest*, or as a reference to *wood*, not *mountain*. The most appropriate and literal Spanish translation of the English word *mountain* is *montaña*. It has a tilde over the last N, making its Spanish pronunciation *mon-tawn-ya*. Turns out the children who grew up in Sierra Madre had liars for parents. I will cut them some slack, though, as I don't believe they had Google Translate when I was growing up in the 1960s. (Fun fact: the tilde, which is part of the Spanish letter ñ, is pronounced *till-duh* in English and *teel-day* in Spanish.)

If the founders of the California town of Sierra Madre wanted it to be named Mother Mountain in Spanish, why didn't they name it *Montaña Madre*? No, for some reason they named it *Mother Saw*.

Let's get to the point of my story, which is my particular pronunciation of certain words, which I had assumed because of where I grew up.

The pronunciation of vowels is slightly different depending on whether you are speaking English with a true Latin influence or a true American influence. When speaking with a true Latin pronunciation, A, E, I, O, and U are pronounced ah, ehh, eee, oh, and ooo.

My learning to read, write, and pronounce words as a kid was influenced by seeing signs written in and hearing people speak in Spanish. I liked it. I liked things that were different. For example, since early childhood I saw and heard many words that included the letter J. I learned which words had silent J's, like Tijuana and Baja, and which words were pronounced with a hard J, like July, injure, and perjury.

When I see words like Lima and Chile, my American English sees them like lie-muh and chill-ee. But as a young teen in So Cal, I knew the true Latin way to pronounce them was *lee*-muh and *chee*-lay.

I remember seeing a video of the pop-rock band the Police playing a concert in South America. Sting said into the microphone, "Great to be here tonight in Chill-ee!" He wasn't worldly and wise yet. He was still in his twenties, so how could he be worldly and wise? Yes, he was skilled at Tantric yoga sex, but he didn't yet know how to pronounce Spanish words. I'm sure he would now greet his fans in Chile with, "Great to be here tonight in Chee-lay!" Then he'd go backstage and have Tantric yoga sex for nine hours.

When I would read books or articles that mentioned the city of Yakima, Washington, I would hear it in my head as Yah-*kee*-ma. In fact, I thought it was pronounced that way until I was in my early twenties, when I met someone who talked about that town and the famous Yakima racks for carrying bicycles and kayaks on a car roof. The person pronounced it *Yack*-uh-maw. I said, "Oh, do you mean Yah-*kee*-ma?" He thought I was trying to be funny. I wasn't. I thought he was an idiot for saying *Yack*-uh-maw.

Similarly, for years I heard people say a certain word when talking about people and food in Louisiana. When I heard them mention these foods or people, I saw it in my mind as *Cagin'*. It made sense to me because I thought it was a reference to an alligator cage. I assumed that this word meant *caging* people and *caging* food. When I read the word *Cajun* in a book or article, I pronounced it Cah-*hoon* in my mind. My Southern California upbringing came into play, and I assumed that the J in Cajun was surely silent and the U was pronounced *ooo*. So, Cajun =

Cah-*hoon*. Not until I was in my early twenties did I learn that the word was pronounced *Cay*-junn.

Throughout my whole life on the West Coast I had read about the almost-mythical Greenwich Village. Among other things, the town was known as the birthplace of the internationally famous folk group Peter, Paul and Mary. (Magically, I have met and become friends with Peter Yarrow. He lives part-time in Telluride, Colorado, where my wife and I live a small part of the year. I'm fascinated by people who pursue their craft to the extent that they become internationally known. I told Peter that I was very big in the heating-and-air-conditioning arena. I said, "Thousands of people pack into stadiums to watch me troubleshoot furnaces and air conditioners!" He chuckled. He's a kind, sweet person.)

I did not travel much as I was coming up through my twenties, thirties, and beyond; I was too damn busy being a hard-working, lots-of-tax-paying, good, obedient American citizen. It wasn't until I was fifty-six years old that I made my first trip to New York City, and I loved it. My wife and I spent ten days there. She was working with a film editor on a project, so I was free to explore the city. I walked and took the subway to many different places. One area that I wanted to check out was the aforementioned Greenwich Village.

Not only had I read about the New York City neighborhood of Greenwich Village, I had also heard people talk about a place called Grenitch Village. As I was trying to find Grenitch Village, I asked a person on the street, "Where is Grenitch Village?" (He was very nice. I didn't experience any rude or impatient people in the whole ten-day trip.) He pointed and told me where to find it. I said, "Thank you. Can you also tell me where to find Green-witch Village?" He started to laugh. I asked why that was funny. He explained there is no Green-witch Village, only "Grenitch" Village. It was then that I learned Green-witch Village and Grenitch Village were the same place.

TRANCE DANCE

I was living in Ashland, Oregon in 2009, happily (and singly) running my HVAC company. The wife of a client had taken it upon herself to try to find a romantic partner for me. What follows is an actual letter I wrote to her.

Hi Kay,

In response to your question whether or not I'm currently courting anyone, no, I'm not dating. I think I have exhausted the crazy midlife single's Rolodex in this town. My last date was with an amicable woman who said, "I can't believe you don't have a girlfriend" and "I have friends who would give their right arm for a guy like you" and "Surely you have them lined up at your door." But she herself declined to line up at my door, and I don't have a collection of female right arms. I never heard from her again.

I simply have not met anyone I am interested in or with whom I have much compatibility. I don't know what to do except give up. I really don't want to date at all but would, of course, love to find *one* wonderful woman and start building a life with her. Why does it seem as if that will never happen? Maybe I have to completely give up hope of ever finding anyone and truly not care anymore. Maybe then the planets will align.

I have met mostly airy-fairy, space-cadet, ungrounded woo-woo types and some who are likely clinically insane. Are the men in this town the same? I shouldn't be so surprised, I mean, there are drum circles every weekend in front of the co-op. And there is Crazy Jen, the topless hardbody bicyclist who rides against animal cruelty. Oh, yeah, I almost forgot Naked Guy, who strolls East Main and Lithia Way wearing only a backpack and Birkenstocks.

The one woman I hoped I might form a great relationship with slowly revealed that she was so severely jealous of everybody and everything that it was like something out of a bad rom-com movie. Once, when we were out of town on a romantic getaway, I accidentally called her by the name of an ex *while we were eating burritos*. She promptly got up, made a scene, and stormed out of the restaurant, then walked several miles to a rental car agency, rented a car, and disappeared for three days. When she finally reappeared, she acted like absolutely nothing had happened.

Another time, we had what appeared to be a pleasant date night of dinner and watching a play at a local theater. At the restaurant, she continuously scanned the room for attractive women. She would alternately fix her gaze on my eyes and then beam in the direction of an attractive woman in order to catch me looking in their direction. On the drive home, she asked me boldly, "At any time during the play, did you imagine yourself having sex with any of the actresses?" I knew that she required a relationship of total transparency, so I wasn't stupid enough to answer in any way but brutal honesty. "Yes, as a matter of fact, I did imagine what it might be like to have sex with the lead actress in the play." She bounced back against the car seat, clapped her hands, and shouted, "See! I knew it! Stop the car! I'll walk home! I can't be with a man who has any thoughts of having sex with other women!" I gathered up my courage and asked, "Never mind just looking, but do you mean I can't ever even *think* about another woman?" She blurted, "Yes! Pull over and stop the F&%$@ing car!" I immediately complied. She quickly got out and slammed the door shut. "Just go! I'll walk." In three days we were back at it, humping like a couple of crazed camels.

I keep hearing the voice of an old Asian man whispering to me, "Choose wisely next time, grasshoppa."

Anyway, Kay, thank you for the invitation to the Trance Dance. Is it this Saturday night? You may have already sent me the info; I'll check my emails. What time? Where? What do I wear? I'm not sure what one would consider appropriate attire for a Trance Dance. A robe? Tie-dye? Should I buy a dreadlocks wig? I already have hairy armpits. :-)

While I've never been to a Trance Dance, I went to a Sunday morning ecstatic dance about three weeks ago. I was invited to go by one of my recent MiddleAgedLookingForLovedotcom incompatibles. After our first date at a local tea house, I was hopeful that we would find something in common. Although we didn't seem to have any sparks to speak of, I agreed to meet her at the ecstatic dance.

That Sunday, I twirled and sweated for over two hours (like a card-carrying Grateful Dead groupie) and did the requisite tumbling and rolling all over other bodies. At the end, all seventeen attendees ended up in a huge "puppy pile" with our limbs intertwined. My chest was still heaving from the aerobic exertion as I lay, unable to free myself from a sea of unshaven legs, underarms, and faces. I ended up stuck in place, like the guy at the bottom of a football tackle pile, my nose pressed against somebody's mouth who had obviously eaten a plate of Greek food prior to arriving at the dance.

Outside, after the puppy pile dispersed, I embraced the woman who had invited me. I wanted to show her that I appreciated her and that I felt we might develop an interest in each other. I'm sure I was a bit high from the ecstasy of all the body touching, and I gave her a nice long hug. After I relaxed my arms and let them fall to my side, she stepped back rather quickly and said, "You hugged me too tightly and held the hug too long. That's a sign that you're going to fall in love with me too quickly. I think we should stop seeing each other." Thank goddess (ha ha!). I avoided what could have ended up being years of singing bowl therapy, silent meditation, and hundreds of raw, cruelty-free, fair trade, boiled leek root dinners with her.

I think I'll just avoid all the airy fairies at the moment. I really do not belong in that world. I have tried to dabble on that side and experience things their way. I observe that whole world and its devotees from the angle of a comedy writer. *This is great stuff to put in a sitcom!* But in our town, it's real.

Let's get back to the Trance Dance. Tell me more. The woman who is leading the event is named Luciphya? Is she really a *mystic muse*? I don't mean to sound disrespectful, but what the hell is that? Ha! I'm playfully teasing, but I really don't know, and I *do* think it's funny.

I must admit that the sound of *Trance Dance* scares me a bit, but if I do go, it would only be to see who I could meet. I wouldn't go if I weren't looking. Normally I would go to something like this *after* I met someone, but only because I loved her. I am simply like that. I do things for the people I love that I wouldn't normally do. In my opinion, a loving partner should come over into the world of one's partner and see what it's all about. My future mate might go with me to some avant-garde or weird music concert I was passionate about, or go watch a motorcycle race (that she might really dislike) at least once because she loved me.

All this to say, I think I just need to leave everything alone for now, just live my life in a neutral place. I'm superbusy with my heating and air business and getting great joy from writing and marketing my songs and playing music. I think I should just do that for now. Sorry!

Thank you so much for thinking of me and finding me worthy of your time.

All the best,

Doug

PS: I just found the Trance Dance flier online and added it below. It's hilarious! Or am I being *insensitive and unevolved* (as one former date told me)? Maybe I'm simply *out of it* and too *square* to understand? Will you hate me if I italicize *one* more word?

Yule greetings!

The old is melting into the Earth and the New Cycle is beckoning us. We are all being stretched to become more of who we truly are. At this activated time, when the old is shaking out and the beautiful and brilliant new energies ignite us, you are invited to dance this amazing shift in a sacred circle. Sacred movement is the most powerful way I have discovered to integrate all the new energies that are pouring through me and to honor all that has been gifted to me.

I will be holding my Annual Winter Solstice Dance Ritual on Sunday. Please join in on an Inward Movement Journey deep into the darkness and the beginning of a new cycle of light! This is a powerful ceremony to honor all that you have been and to open to the gifts that are coming.

To pre-register, please call or email by December 20 (details below).

Solstice Blessings to all!

Dance with the Divine Spark!

You are invited on a journey into the Divine Darkness of the Winter Solstice. Enter the Womb of Darkness. Honor Your Walk this year. Embody the Spark of Creation. Drink the Divine Nectar of your Essence. Ground in the New. Dance with the Divine is an Ancient, Sacred, and Powerful personal practice. Please bring a pillow and a bandanna or scarf. Offerings for the altar are welcome.

This is a Sacred Ceremony. Please be on time.

(Note from the author: Please be sure, dear reader, to check out the Lucky Doug Fergus songs "Stop, Drop and Roll" and "Love Tank," available on all digital music platforms. They were written in response to the interactions I had in real life, as outlined in this story.)

SAINT PETRA AND HER PEARLY GATES

Hi. My name is Saint Petra. My father, Saint Peter, passed on to level 2 of the afterlife a while ago. He was home in Heaven watching reruns of *I Love Lucy* when he died from a laughing attack during the scene where Lucy and Ethel were at the conveyor belt in the candy factory. (Yes, we have TV in the afterlife, but only two shows: *I Love Lucy* and a house-flipping show hosted by an impossibly good-looking woman and a dorky, average-looking man.) Soon after Dad went to level 2, I got his old job of Heaven's gatekeeper, interviewing and scrutinizing all incomers to Heaven. I now live in level 1 of the afterlife.

My life in Heaven had been fun when I was young, living among the clouds as the child of an angel, but Dad sent me down to Earth so I could have a typical human experience and be a considerate and compassionate gatekeeper should I ever desire to apply for that position. (He had hopes that I would take over his job after he retired.)

On Earth, I was married to a mostly wonderful man, Lozario Lozario Lozario. (You've heard of those people whose first and last names are the same? Try being married to a man with *three* same names. Lozario Lozario Lozario required me and everyone in his inner circle to always address him using all three. I wasn't allowed to give him a cute nickname, like Lozee or Loz-a-reenie or Lozzie and the Jets.)

We were faithful to each other, but when I was in my forties I had the desire to experience another woman's physical passion. It was purely so that I could better prepare for when I was gatekeeper. I wanted to have a better comprehension of the lifestyle so that when lesbians and bisexual women arrived at the gate, I wouldn't prejudge them negatively. Lozario Lozario Lozario and I divorced for three months the year I was forty-six. I had a couple of short-term flings with other women, made notes in my journal, then remarried Lozario Lozario Lozario.

As is typical for many adult humans, we had two kids, and I tried the best I could to help them develop into positively contributing adults. I wanted the mothering experience mostly so that, again, I could be a more considerate and compassionate gatekeeper. I did not feel that Lozario Lozario Lozario was my soul mate nor that my kids were the best kids ever.

I was a dental hygienist for thirty-four years while I raised our little munchkins. Thirty-four years of smelling stinky mouths and hearing people give the lamest excuses for being late or not showing up at all. Every day I had to make small talk with people I didn't really care about, listening to their mundane, trite, proletarian, banal, vapid, hackneyed, insipid, plebeian, and tedious banter. (And yes, those *were* the names of the male strippers at Hunk-O-Mania on Yucca Street in Los Angeles.) I could hardly wait to go home each day because Lozario Lozario Lozario and I had a passionate hobby of building and driving monster trucks through muddy fields behind our house.

Lozario Lozario Lozario considered a career of stealing, lying, and cheating; making stupid, insensitive, racist, homophobic, misogynistic, derogatory statements; and telling outright fabrications to climb the ladder of success, but he decided to reject the life of a politician and sell feather dusters door to door instead. After my time on Earth was up and Dad decided I should go back up to cloud life, I was in Heaven. The first cloud house I lived in when I came back was in a cool, hip section of Heaven. There were funky coffee shops, groovy street musicians, and those oddballs who dress and paint themselves to look like a statue and hold very, very still. I loved sitting on my stoop, playing my vinyl collection of Joni Mitchell, Bonnie Raitt, Judy Collins, Bootsy Collins, James Brown, Jackson Browne, Diana Ross, Rick Ross, and Rickie Lee Jones albums. I would pretend that I was the reigning queen of popular music. (I know this could be my reality if I lost thirty pounds, were forty years younger, took singing lessons, got my teeth whitened, and had another chance on Earth.)

After a while, I got bored just lazing about all day, drinking green tea, reading romance novels, eating grapes (I had to hold the bunch myself, so don't go thinking I had a group of hunky, oiled-up musclemen to hold them for me), and practicing the harp (I'm awful! I don't think I'll ever be any good), and I started thinking about applying for Dad's old job. I was also tired of dwelling on the fact that some of my friends had better cloud houses than I did. Even though I knew that envy and covetousness were frowned upon, I couldn't shake off my envious yearning. In fact, some people thought my hankering for better housing would automatically disqualify me for the gatekeeper job, but I suppose that I was allowed to apply because of who Dad was. Although I loved living in that cool, hip section of Heaven, if I got the job, I would look forward to moving to the gatekeeper section, where property values were higher (according to Zillow).

I was excited when my application was accepted and an interview was scheduled. In the week before my interview, I cleared my head each morning by performing asanas from several different yoga disciplines: Oh Yessa, Ash-Tango, and my favorite, Make-My-Hair-Shiny-And-Thick-Again. I really wanted to be a gatekeeper because I liked the idea of sizing people up and deciding whether they had lived lives worthy enough to be admitted into Heaven. You already know I got the job because I told you that in the first paragraph. Now, every day as I commute in my cloud car to the Gates, my mind is flooded with good thoughts that I'm making a difference in the Universal Karmic Cosmos by sincerely and respectfully giving a thorough interrogation to every spirit that arrives. (If you're wondering what a cloud car looks like, think of a Flintstones car but made of clouds.)

If you would like to know what it's like to be a gatekeeper of the pearly kind, you can read some of the interesting experiences I have had in the following stories.

STORY 1

Petra: Hello there, new arrival! Welcome to Saint Petra's Pearly Gates. For security purposes, please give me your username and password.

Arrival: I don't think I have a username and password yet, do I?

Petra: You didn't go to double-you double-you double-you dot heaven dot com and register as a new user?

Arrival: No, sorry!

Petra: No prob. We'll take care of it. I have to ask you some questions before I can let you in, though. What was your contribution to society on Earth?

Arrival: Oh, I didn't know I was supposed to make any kind of contribution. I was just a person who worked, watched TV, ate, and pooped.

Petra: Were you happy?

Arrival: Yes! I loved my life.

Petra: Well, I suppose that *could* qualify as a contribution, considering that the energy of your happiness likely rubbed off on others.

Arrival: That's nice that you say my happiness *could* qualify, but what should I have done that absolutely *would* have qualified as a contribution?

Petra: In no particular order: coin, stamp, and

baseball card collecting. Trying to find a cure for cancer. Taking a dog for a walk. Reading poetry to inmates at a prison. Being a fastidious dishwasher. Being cheerful and friendly to strangers. Learning and practicing a musical instrument or a form of art. It could even be something like, when you want to stop a microwave oven before the timer is done, you *press the cancel button* instead of leaving it with fourteen seconds on the timer for the next person.

Arrival: Oh. I never did any of those things. I often stopped the microwave early and didn't press the cancel button. I didn't like the loud beep sound it made. Why beep five times in a row, anyway?

Petra: Tsk, tsk.

Arrival: I've always assumed that Heaven is free of conflict. Is there any arguing or anxiety up here? And are people mostly smart and interesting? Or is everyone mellow as the month of May?

Petra: If you envisioned everyone sitting around eating cloud-based cotton candy while smiling at each other and chatting about the weather, Heavens to Betsy, no! Heaven knows that would be boring.

Arrival: How about those of us who are single and want to mingle?

Petra: Keep in mind that by the time you arrive here, biological urges have dissipated into the stratosphere. You can flirt all you want, but no one will respond. They'll simply think you're a funny weirdo and give you a cute name like Humper.

Arrival: Good to know. So, when I *do* tease and act

like a coquettish filly, I won't offend anyone or embarrass myself.

Petra: Sheesh-a-Maria! It takes all kinds.

STORY 2

Petra: Hello, new arrival. Welcome to the fabulous Pearly Gates! How was your trip?

Arrival: Basically—

Petra: —No, no. We don't start sentences with *basically* here in Heaven.

Arrival: Um, okay.

Petra: Oh, boy, here we go again. Please, no *um* either. Do you have any questions before we begin the interview process?

Arrival: Yes, I sure do. What is coleet dust?

Petra: Huh?

Arrival: "Warm smell of coleet dust, rising up through the air."

Petra: Ohhh, that song. "Hotel California." I have no idea. I've been wondering about that myself for decades. Here's one I've never been able to figure out. In that song, "I'd Really Love to See You Tonight," why does he sing, "I'm not talking about the *linen*"?

Arrival: I have no idea. I thought you would know.

Petra: I can't know everything! But I do know that I love you. And I know that if you love me too, what a wonderful world this would be.

Arrival: Cute, Saint Petra, cute. Sam Cooke?

Petra: Yes. He's been here since 1964. You might

occasionally find him walking his dog on Paradisiacal Place.

Arrival: Oh! So dogs are allowed in Heaven?

Petra: Yes, but only the good ones. No bad, mean dogs here. So yes, If you had a nice dog on Earth, you'll be reunited with it. The bonus is that they don't poop anymore. No more picking up the darn doo-doo!

Arrival: Now that we're on the subject of animals and such, can you talk to Mother Nature about redesigning the look of spiders? If she would make them look like kittens, we wouldn't be afraid of them.

Petra: But then how would we tell the difference between kittens and spiders?

Arrival: We could design the new spiders to have a big S on their backs and kittens would have a big K.

Petra: What about people who speak another language and have different words for kitten and spider or have a different alphabet altogether?

Arrival: Smarty pants.

Petra: Well, I *did* have to pass a review to get this job, and I *did* beat out many other applicants.

Arrival: Speaking of other languages, how do you interpret when non-English-speaking people arrive?

Petra: I am conversational in all languages. I can immediately adapt and speak the native language of any new arrival.

Arrival: I hear you say that you can speak at a *conversational level* in all languages, but what if a person arrives from, say, Pakistan and wants to discuss complex subjects with you, like the volatile situation in the Middle West?

Petra: I just nod and alternate between saying, "That's nice, I'm sorry, good for you, and I'll try."
Arrival: Interesting. By the way, your voice is curiously familiar. You sound like someone I've heard before. Someone I've heard a lot, actually, but I can't quite put my finger in it.
Petra: You mean you can't quite put your finger *on* it?
Arrival: Yes, right. *On* it.
Petra: Well, let's move on.
Arrival: No, wait. It's coming to me. I've got it! You're the voice of Siri. Am I right?!
Petra: What on earth—I mean in Heaven—are you saying?
Arrival: Oh, I know what you're up to. You're the shy type. Or maybe you're sworn to secrecy, like the actress Laura Linney, who isn't supposed to tell anyone that she's the voice of NPR. Am I right?
Petra: *ahem* It says here that you were a businessperson.
Arrival: Yes, I was the founder and editor-in-chief of *Failed Entrepreneur* magazine. I made millions from selling advice to people who tried and tried but never became successful. Before that, I targeted my advice to smart, upwardly mobile achievers. But as soon as they understood my business principles, they would cancel their subscriptions to my magazine, and stop buying my books and attending my seminars. So I shifted gears and sought out a new client base of dumb-dumbs.
Petra: Where did all these "dumb-dumbs" come from?
Arrival: They were all adult paintball players.

Petra: I see. Any more questions?

Arrival: I sure do! I have tons of them. Who's the most popular singer here in Heaven? Elvis?

Petra: Of course not. He's still alive.

Arrival: What do you mean he's still alive? He died in 1977.

Petra: Oh, *that* Elvis. I thought you were talking about Costello.

Arrival: Lou Castello from the comedy team of Abbott and Costello?

Petra: No, silly, *Elvis* Costello.

Arrival: "Ohhh, is that how you pronounce it? All these decades I've been saying it in Spanish, *Co-stay-o.*"

Petra: Tell me about any contributions you made to the people of Earth.

Arrival: I was the inventor of the left-handed guitar pick and the metric adjustable wrench.

Petra: I think you have a deep love for your dumb-dumbs. Do I sense that you are a bit of a dumb-dumb yourself?

Arrival: I don't like your tone, Petra.

Petra: *Saint* Petra! And *I'm* the one who likes or dislikes a tone of voice, not you.

Arrival: Okay, Okay! Sorry, Saint Petra.

Petra: Be careful there, bub! Now, let me see . . . hmmm . . . it says here that when you flew in a passenger plane, you habitually unbuckled your seat belt before the airplane came to a complete stop.

Arrival: Oops.

Petra: And I see that you never set the parking brake on your car, not even on hills.

Arrival: Yep, real men don't set the parking brake.

Petra: That's just stupid.

Arrival: I understand that *now*. I was a typical macho man. I thought people who were obsessed with safety were sissies. Parking brake, schmarking brake! Then one day I stopped my truck to get the letters out of my mailbox. I left the engine running but forgot to put the transmission in park. I was a few steps from the door when I noticed the truck was rolling, so I made a dive and tried to jump in, but I slipped. I fell down and rolled under the truck. The rear tire ran over me and, well, here I am.

Petra: I can see the headline now: Macho Man Refuses to Set Brake. Wins a Trip to Pearly Gates.

Arrival: I hope you'll let me in, but I have another question. Here in Heaven, do men still compare body parts, like biceps, calves, and penises? It's exhausting, this constant envious worry that we're not big enough or strong enough. I'd like to be able to look at another guy and simply think, *Gosh, I'd love to have a cup of tea with him and talk about lawn seeding techniques, auto parts, and vintage photography.*

Petra: Relax. In Heaven no one compares or is even aware of body parts anymore.

Arrival: Oh, good! I have one more question. *Tengo una pregunta más.*

Petra: Very good. *Muy bueno.* You're showing off your Spanish. I wish more people would learn a second language and travel to interact with other cultures. What's your question?

Arrival: Who's the clown who invented *there, their, they're* and *wear, where, ware*?

Petra: Ya know, that has bugged me for centuries!

STORY 3

Woman appearing at the Pearly Gates: That was certainly a wild ride!

Petra: Hello, new arrival. I'm glad that you're in a good frame of mind. What is your name?

New Arrival: Beatrice Hathaway Plenitude. I was one of the top theater actresses of my time. I never got married or had children so that I could devote all my energy to perfecting my craft and developing my God-given gift to its highest potential.

Petra: I see. Glad to have you. We have many of you folks here. I hope you'll take advantage of our dialogue bank.

Beatrice: Dialogue bank?

Petra: Yes. As you know, all actors spend most of their time and energy memorizing dialogue. But where does all that dialogue go after the production is over? Poof! Gone forever. It was such a shame to let it all vaporize into the ether, so we started capturing all of it. We created a dialogue bank here in Heaven. It contains the actual sound recordings from every theater production since we started the project in 1834.

Beatrice: Fascinating! I can relive thousands of glorious moments from my incredible career as one of the top—no, I dare say, *the* top actress of my time.

Petra: When I was on Earth, I was quite good in my school drama class, but I didn't make a career of it. I was—I mean I *am*—a proud dental hygienist, but I always wondered if I could have made it as an actress. May I give you a little sample of my ability?

Beatrice: Please go ahead.

Petra: "Four score, eleven months, two weeks and three days ago, great men tiptoed surreptitiously while searching for purposefulness in forbidden forests of carob bean and banana plants, trembling with trepidation. It was common knowledge that staggering buffalo moccasins could light upon a brittle twig or dry leaf and awaken the bright recesses of our neighbors' minds and inform the rapacious inhabitants of our planet Claire." Thank you.

Beatrice: Saint Petra! I like it! You are quite good.

Petra: You're just being polite, aren't you?

Beatrice: Yes. But don't feel bad, Saint Petra. I attended the Julienne School of Acting and Potato Preparation on a full scholarship. I studied for many years with top teachers. I've mastered the Stan-Never-Liked-Coleslaw-Or-Learned-To-Ski method, the Whoopee-Straw-Little-Town method, the Cluck-Off method, and the Owen Wilson I-Don't-Act-I-Just-Play-Myself-In-Every-Movie method. So of course you aren't equal in acting skill to me.

Petra: I see. We are certainly full of ourselves, aren't we?

Beatrice: I'm sorry for being honest. I assume you value honesty here in Heaven?

Petra: Listen here, missy. You wouldn't last a day as a dental hygienist. If you're so smart, tell me what I should do if a patient has an occlusional disruptive fragmentation of the tissue surrounding the twenty-third bicuspid when the twenty-fourth tricuspid is verging on a rotational merge axis with an intersectional ratio of 65:89?

Beatrice: Hmmm. Well, first I would cross-collateralize the area adjacent to the sixteenth incisor if, and only if, the regional plateau of Cortez has suffered a shifting of its companionability. If so, I would proceed with Myrtle's law of hypotropic subextrication.

Petra: So you would tie one end of a string to the tooth, the other end to a doorknob, then slam the door?

Beatrice: Yes.

Petra: Okay. You win. You're a better actress *and* hygienist than I. Come on in! But first, tell me if I'm funny. I have an acting joke I made up in 1956, when I was 335 years old. "Carol was in a group of traveling theater actors. To avoid getting motion sickness on the bus, she took Dramamine."

Beatrice: Ha! That is truly funny and clever, Saint Petra!

Petra: Oh, Beatrice. Thank you.

Beatrice: Before I come in, I want to talk about a concern I have for my fellow humans still living on Earth and the obvious overpopulation. I mean, why are people still having babies? There isn't enough water, clean air, and food for everyone as it stands now. In fact, the production of cute, furry living creatures that are slaughtered for protein produces more excrement than meat! And why did the designer of the human body make the sex act so gosh darn pleasurable? It's no wonder the Earth is overpopulated! The sex act should be a tedious experience.

Petra: It is for most women.

Beatrice: Ha, funny, Saint Petra!

Petra: I'm not being funny.

Beatrice: I won't disagree with you on that. In my opinion, the sex act should hurt. It should be painful enough that teenage boys will masturbate only once a month instead of four or five times a day. The thought of having sex should give girls a massive headache.

Petra: For many, it does.

Beatrice: Maybe we can redesign the male body so that when he thrusts his hips forward, it will feel like a knife is being jabbed into his spine.

Petra: Wow, Beatrice. That seems harsh, doesn't it? If that were the case, men would have a hard time dancing.

Beatrice: They could still move their hips side to side. Just no thrusting forward.

Petra: But women could still get pregnant using the woman-on-top method.

Beatrice: I hadn't thought of that. Darn. What if we redesigned the female body so that the reproductive area was not developed until they were forty years old? No opening, like Barbie!

Petra: In that case, a woman who had a baby at forty would be fifty-seven when their kid graduated from high school. Is that okay with you?

Beatrice: Sure! That way all babies would be carefully planned. We should phase out this idiocy of girls being able to get pregnant at what, fourteen, fifteen. Certainly not before they are twenty-five.

Petra: I hear you and will carefully consider this idea. Now, do you have any more questions for me before you come through the gate?

Beatrice: I've always been an inquisitive person. I believe that's why I was the top actor—

Petra: —*of your time*. I know!

Beatrice: Sheesh, Saint Petra, you don't have to raise your voice. Why don't mattresses have handles on them anymore? Who is the lamebrain who created popcorn ceiling texture in homes? Is it *jury*-rigged or *jerry*-rigged? What's wrong with people who don't like the taste of cilantro? If water has to be at 212 degrees Fahrenheit to boil, then how does it evaporate at room temperature? What useful purpose do hiccups serve? Why did God make it so that we breathe, drink, and eat through the same hole? Shouldn't the air intake hole be on the top of the head and the mouth only for eating and drinking?

Petra: I hear you, Beatrice, but you have too many questions for now. You will find your answers in due time. Maybe you can tell me why some people say *ree-litor* instead of *real-tor* and *joo-lery* instead of *jewel-ry*?

Beatrice: Right! I can't help you there.

Petra: Maybe we'll both find out on the next episode of *As Heaven Turns*.

Beatrice: Does Heaven have Tuesday Trivia Game

Night? How about Pizza Friday at work? What time of day does the mail get delivered? I have a very particular bowel elimination routine every morning. Will I get my own private bathroom?

Petra: We don't eat or shit anymore here in Heaven— oops, sorry. I mean *poop*.

Beatrice: Isn't that a line from a Bee Gees song? "Nobody poops much in Heaven no more."

Petra: That's funny. You're remarkably witty.

Beatrice: Are you saying that just to be polite?

Petra: No. I mean it. We can use more people like you. I'm going to place you in the trades people's neighborhood. You'll add some sparkle and shine to your block of plumbers, electricians, HVAC techs, drywall installers, house painters and copy machine repair people.

Beatrice: Oh boy. Thanks.

STORY 4

Hello, dear reader. You are welcome to observe today's transactions if you'd like. There's a chair on the far side over there; have a seat. Please excuse me. I see someone at the gate. It's a woman who is about forty-five years old. She's disheveled and bewildered. That's never a good sign. (Hey! *Disheveled and Bewildered.* Band name!)

Petra: Hello, welcome to Heaven. My name is Saint Petra. How may I help you?

Woman: Um, uh, I think I'm lost. Maybe I took a wrong turn somewhere.

(I wish humans would stop saying *um* and *uh*. Do you agree, dear reader? It's really not necessary. Just leave space and silence, right? Answers on a postcard.)

Petra: No, you're not lost. You're right where you're supposed to be.

Woman: Uh, I don't think so. Um, I was only forty-five when I died.

Petra: I'm sorry. But before we continue, I have to ask you to please refrain from saying *um* and *uh*. Can you do that?

Woman: That's a weird request. Okay?

Petra: Are you saying *okay* with a question mark? Or do you agree to stop saying *um* and *uh*?

Woman: I'll try.

Petra: There is no try, there is only do. Look, it's not okay, okay? Okay, let me look at my clipboard. Hmmm. It says here that you died of cancer.

Woman: Yes, but I ate blueberries and dark chocolate! I had weekly colon irrigations of pomegranate juice/paprika/coffee/ginger pulp and pine sap! I drank organic bison bone broth and ate kale! I mean *lots* of kale! Five pounds a day! I put it in smoothies with oat milk, avocado, almond butter, nutritional yeast, flax seed meal, and cactus root protein powder! I nearly went broke buying all that stuff!

Petra: I'm sorry to inform you that you could have just eaten bologna on white bread sandwiches with potato chips. All those costly ingredients had no effect on your cancer.

Woman: You aren't stretching my chain, are you?

Petra: Of course not! I'm Saint Petra. Would I—how did you say it—*stretch your chain*?

Woman: No, I didn't think you would. I must say that I've heard a lot about you over the years that I was alive on the Earth.

Petra: Really? Who talked about me?

Woman: My 128-year-old cat, who died in November 1873, when I was a child of nine. Dear Fluffy said most everyone loved you and that you were a fair and impartial gate marshal.

Petra: That's nice of Fluffy to say. What kind of cancer did you die from?

Woman: It doesn't say on your clipboard there?

Petra: That wasn't sarcastic, was it?

Woman: No, ma'am. I passed on from acute, luke-enema caprese-tacoma my-eyelid limpo-bastic truckcinoma astro-cyclops, gastro-infrequent drip with a maligned fibrous, hysterical, rubba-dubba, infusional, tuma-creatic, hodgepodge-cousin, go-longio and catchit of the left pinky toe.

Petra: Ooh, ouch! I'm sorry. There really is no rhyme or reason for that. It wasn't "God's plan" or any of that nonsense. God doesn't actually need more people up here. No offense, but God didn't "take" you so that you could be of better service in Heaven. That's a silly myth.

I know it's hard to comprehend now, but really, all that kale you ate had no effect on preventing cancer, sorry (unless it was Jim Gaffigan Signature Kale available only at Costco stores in the United States). After carefully considering your case, I can find only one strike against you.

Woman: Do you mean they know about the time I carelessly dropped an orange peel on the ground in the desert of Moab, Utah, thereby putting foreign vegetable matter in a non-native habitat?

Petra: Hold on, I'm writing. No. That wasn't it. It was your annoying practice of using a ballpoint pen until it stopped writing and then not scribbling circles on a piece of paper to get a few more sentences out of it. You immediately tossed the pen in the trash and got out a new one.

Woman: Oops. Sorry. I'll try to be better.

Petra: We don't have ballpoint pens in Heaven. You can't *be better* about it.

Woman: Oh, right.

Petra: I only mention this in the event that you are reincarnated and go back to Earth as a human. If that happens, I suggest that you use the scribbling-circles-on-scratch-paper method to extract all of the precious ink from your pens before you throw them away. We have enough plastic trash in our soils and oceans without you prematurely tossing your pens.

Woman: Wait. Did you say *reincarnated*?

Petra: I did. I said *in the event* that you are reincarnated.

Woman: Does ... does that mean ... does that mean I'm not going ... *down there*?

Petra: It does!

Woman: Oh, Petra! I love you!

Petra: Now, now. *Saint* Petra.

Woman: Right! *Saint* Petra! You are the best saint ever!

STORY 5

There are three characters in this story: I, Saint Petra, am the main character. Then we have Gull Able, a man in his early thirties, and his seven-year-old daughter, Cutie Pie.

Gull is looking through the bars of the Pearly Gates.

Gull: Hellooo. Is anybody there?

Petra: Please be patient. I'm 347 years old. I'm hurrying.

Gull: Sorry.

Petra: All right, and who do we have here?

Gull: My name is Gull. Gull Able.

Petra: I'm guessing you were thirty-two-ish years old.

Gull: Close. Thirty-one.

Petra: Oh, gosh! I see an adorable child with you! Who might this be?

Gull: This is my daughter, Cutie Pie. She was seven years old.

Petra: Oh, my lord. What happened? Canoe capsized? Trapped in a burning house? Got flung out off your seats on a Ferris wheel at the amusement park?

Gull: Nope. None of those. We're from Florida. I put a Yamaha 250 engine in my riding lawn mower. I built a ramp out of plywood, took my little Cutie Pie here on my lap, and tried to jump the lawn mower over the barn.

Petra: Oh shit. Oops! Sorry! I'm not supposed to say those kinds of words. I'm a saint, after all.

Cutie Pie: It's all right. That's what Cooter, Scooter, Pooter, Bobbi Clem, and Winnie Jack said when we crashed and landed upside down on the roof of the neighbor's house and came to our final resting place in the kitchen while the lady of the house was making 'possum gut pie.

Petra: You sure know how to go out in style! But darn it, Gull. I don't like that you took little Cutie Pie here with you. That weren't too smart—I mean, that wasn't very smart.

Gull: I'm truly sorry about the whole incident. If I could do it over, I'd install a Yamaha 450 engine. I'm sure we would have cleared the neighbor's house and landed in the pond, as I had hoped we would.

Petra: I don't think you've learned a thing.

Gull: I'm not disputing that I should be here instead of back on Earth, Miss Petra.

Petra: That's *Saint*—wait. I kind of like Miss Petra. Carry on.

Gull: I hope I've done enough good, or that you'll at least find I had good intentions, and let us stay here in Heaven. I'd rather not be split from my little Cutie Pie.

Petra: You have a good point. If I send you *down there* and she stays here, she may experience abandonment issues. Let me look over your information here on my clipboard. Oh, here's something of note. It says that soon after email became a widespread, common way for people to communicate, circa 1997, you started using that wonderful new communication system only for bombarding your friends, family, and coworkers with stupid, moronic jokes and cartoons. Everyone got sick of your emails and dreaded receiving any electronic communications from you. No one wanted to hurt your precious feelings, but finally a cute husband and wife, Brian and Maggie, whom you met at a convention for 1950s-era comic books and vintage steam-powered sewing machines, conjured up the nerve to send you an email asking you to please take them off your mailing list. You were predictably offended and wrote them a reply. Do you remember this?

Gull: Vaguely.

Petra: I have a copy here on my clipboard. I'll read it to you.

Hello Brian and Maggie,
 I'll never speak to you again because you asked me to not send you fun emails anymore. I've been so upset by this that I've developed mental and physical (even psychic!) sores and other odd symptoms. My doctor has put me on special diets and movement programs in order to find the root cause, but I know what is wrong. YOU TWO are the root cause! You squelched my creative juicery! I firmly believe that Al Gore's invention (the Internet) was brought to me for the express purpose of allowing me to share my funny worldview with the rest of the planet. The main manifestation of your spurning my comedic outpouring has been that I have not been able to swallow solid food for six weeks. My doctor has devised a special liquid diet that is my only source of happiness now. Once

a day, a nurse pours a quart of the following slop down my alimentary canal: nonfat hazelberry yogurt, wheat germ, wheat grass, wheat bran, Wheaties, nutritional yeast, glass blowers' yeast, basket weavers' yeast, carob chips, and sun-dried lizard toenails. Yum! (Not!)
    I hope to see you both soon. (Not!)
Your only (former) friend,
Gull

Gull: Oh, darn. Did I *really* write that?

Petra: You most certainly did. I had my EET (Email Eavesdropping Team) send me a copy when they discovered it.

Gull: That's embarrassing. I'm sorry.

Petra: Don't be! I mention it because Brian and Maggie found it odd, cool, and amusing. They printed it out and put it on their refrigerator door. It gave them a chuckle every time they walked into their kitchen. That letter earned you one point in the Heaven category.

Gull: Oh, cool! How about that, Cutie Pie?

Cutie Pie: Dad, it's weird, but it's also great that we get one Heaven point for it.

Petra: Let's carry on with your interview. It says here that you, Gull, lived in a state that required front and rear license plates on all automobiles, yet you never installed the front license plate on any of the cars you owned.

Gull: It was unnecessary and a waste of time.

Petra: Gull! Why do you think the DMV issued two plates? Sheesh-a-Maria.

Cutie Pie: Daaaaad!

Petra: Gull, you owned five different cars over the years. What did you do with the front license plates that you never installed?

Gull: I hung them on the wall of my garage-slash-workshop, next to my posters of Snap-on tools girls in bikinis.

Petra: I see. You put the license plates up on the inside of your garage-slash-workshop along with the Snap-on tools posters, thinking it made you . . . what? Cool?

Gull: Sorry, but yes, it felt cool that I had owned five cars, and the pictures of the girls made me feel glad to be alive.

Cutie Pie: Daaaad! You're *so* weird.

Petra: Hmmm. Did you think that every time someone came to visit you in your garage-slash-workshop, they would look at the plates and think, *Oh wow, he's such a macho rebel! He never installed the front license plates on his cars and instead put them up next to the posters of Snap-on bikini models holding tools!*

Gull: Yep. What's wrong with posters of Snap-on tool girls?"

Petra: Hey, they're not *girls*, they're *women*. Girls are under eighteen years old. Women are eighteen years old and older. You'd better not have had posters of *girls* wearing bikinis on your wall. Here, wait a minute. Let me check my notes. Okay, you're in luck. The models were all over eighteen.

Cutie Pie: Hey, Dad?

Gull: What is it, Cutie Pie?

Cutie Pie: Are you sure we're related?

Gull: Why do you say that?

Cutie Pie: You've done some really embarrassing stuff! Maybe we *should* go our separate ways.

Gull: Oh, come on, Cutie Pie! I'm not that bad, am I?

Petra: Here's something interesting from the clipboard. It's a biggie. Not good.

Cutie Pie: Oh, no! Daaaaad! What did he do, Saint Petra?

Petra: Well, Cutie Pie, when he was seven years old, your father stole Snickers candy bars, Topps bubble gum baseball cards, and Hot Wheels toy cars from Toy and Patio Village in Sierra Madre. And not just once but several times.

Cutie Pie: Daaaaad! You were *my* age when you did that?!

Gull: Oh, Cutie Pie. I'm really sorry, but boys are different! Boys are born with a strong desire to break, smash, vandalize, and steal!

Cutie Pie: Now wait a minute. Isn't Break, Smash, Vandalize, and Steal the name of a law firm on 41st Street in New York?

Petra: Ha ha ha! Cutie Pie, that was funny!

Cutie Pie: Thank you, Saint Petra. I'll be here . . . *forever.*

Petra: Actually, Cutie Pie, I'm changing my decision. Your father may remain here, but you are too cool and too young to stay. I'm going to send you back.

Cutie Pie: Really! Oh my gosh, Saint Petra! Thank you! Will I go back as a horse or a cat or maybe a Singer model #4452 sewing machine?

Petra: No, Cutie Pie. You'll go back as your sweet self.

Gull: Look at her. She's ecstatic to go back and leave me here!

Cutie Pie: Daaaad. You had your chance on Earth. Don't you want me to have a chance, too?

Gull: Oh, Cutie Pie. Yes, I *guess*. I mean, of course! Go on! Have fun, and be nice. Stay away from boys with riding lawn mowers.

Petra: Funny, Gull.

Gull: Thanks. I'll be here all week. No—I'll be here... *forever*!

STORY 6

Petra: Hello, new arrival. I'm Saint Petra. This interview may be videotaped for quality and training purposes. What is your name?

New Arrival: Langford da Louse.

Petra: What was your job on Earth, Langford?

Langford da Louse: I was a postal clerk for a while, but dat was just a cover. I was a full-time crinimal. I didn't have no Plan B. I didn't have no passionate hobby. I didn't secretly want to be no songwriter, race car driver, or sewage treatment plant water tester.

Petra: Langford, you should say *any* instead of *no*. And you were a *criminal*.

Langford da Louse: Sorry, Saint Petra. I could never rememba dat gramma stuff. I ain't no Linguine-ist. But I *do* like Italian noodles. And yeah, like I said, I was a crinimal.

Petra: Okay, before we continue, I've always wanted to know something. You were a postal clerk, right?

Langford da Louse: Yeah, fer a coupla years. It was a *front*, see. A *cover*. I was assigned to intra-cept and re-routify soitain valuable packages before dey arrived at deir original, intended desecration.

Petra: All right, so you might know the answer to this question. Why was it that every time I was in line at the post office, it seemed that as the line grew longer, the clerks would close their windows and leave, one by one! A typical scene was a line of fifteen people waiting and only one stone-faced, rude, condescending clerk! Why?

Langford da Louse: Ohhh . . . ha ha! Dat's a secret. Sorry, I can't tells ya why. If I did, I'd have ta—

Petra: —kill me, right?

Langford da Louse: Right!

Petra: I have to tell you that this interview is not going very well for you. I'm looking on my clipboard, and oh boy. You've done a lot of bad stuff! For starters, it says here that you would say, "Top a' da marnin' to ya, missy" in a poorly done fake Irish accent every time you greeted a young woman on a bus, subway, or sidewalk. It was never funny, and the women felt uncomfortable and thought you were mildly creepy. That's a strike against you.

Langford da Louse: Ah, dang it. Sorry 'bout dat. I hadn't evolved yet. I wouldn't do dat now, I tells ya. I'd be respeckable to dem ladies if'n I gots da chance to retoin to Oith.

Petra: Let's keep perusing this clipboard sheet. Bank robberies, counterfeit checks and cash, insurance fraud, and stuffing potatoes in car exhaust pipes. It says here that you started out as an apprentice gangster and that you broke people's arms and kneecaps for nonpayment of extraordinarily high high-interest loans. Is that correct?

Langford da Louse: Yeah. I'm ashamed of it now. I was young, dumb, and fulla—

Petra: I get it! That's no excuse, though. Those incidents of hurting people show you have no empathy.

Langford da Louse: No, I do! Well, I *did*. I always kept some empathy in my refrigerator at home. Ooh, I loved empathy with tomato sauce and demaggio cheese!

Petra: Please don't try to be funny.

Langford da Louse: I wasn't. Whatta youse talkin' 'bout?

Petra: Okay, Langford. The interview is over. I'm sorry to say that I'm sending you *down there*.

Langford da Louse: No no no! Please, Petra, doll face!

Petra: *Saint* Petra, doll face!

Langford da Louse: Right, *Saint* Petra. Please take a look at da clipboid. Shoily you'll find some good tings I done?

Petra: All right, I'll look at the other pages here. Hmmm. Oh, now this is interesting.

Langford da Louse: What's dat? What's inneresting?

Petra: Here on page fourteen. Evidently, you were ordered to *bump off* a woman by the cliché method of concrete boots and then dump her in a lake.

Langford da Louse: Oh, yeah, I rememba dat time.

Petra: Tell me about it, and I'll see if your story coincides with what is written here.

Langford da Louse: I got a call from da boss dat I needed to lie my hands on a lady.

Petra: You mean *lay* your hands on a lady.

Langford da Louse: Dat's right, I went to her 'partment to lie my hands on her.

Petra: No, *lay*. *Lay* your hands on her. Seventy-five percent of English-speaking people say *lie* when they mean *lay* and *lay* when they mean *lie*. You needed to *lay* your hands on that lady.

Langford da Louse: Ya darn right, I did! She was a looka! But da boss tol' me, no hanky panky. Just get da job done.

Petra: Uh-huh, I see.

Langford da Louse: Any whozit, dis lady, she snitched on Grumpy Gregory for when he electronically siphoned off da retirement savings of everyone in Sunny Times Are Ending Soon old folks home.

Petra: Pardon me for noticing, but you have a lot of trouble speaking proper English, yet you easily pronounced *electronically siphoned*.

Langford da Louse: Yeah, I'm one a' dem savants. I got dat *butt sandwich* syndrome.

Petra: Do you mean Asperger's?

Langford da Louse: Uh, no tanks, it don't sound too tasty.

Petra: Please carry on with your story.

Langford da Louse: So I gets da lady and takes her to da hideout. I ties her up, and puts each a' her feet in a bucket. I starts mixin' da concrete, and I starts tinkin' dat she's a lady, ya know? A goil. So I decides I just can't do it. I mean, we all come from goils, right? My muddah was a goil. I get in my cah, and I drives to da mall, to da Michael's aht supply place. I gets me two big blocks a dat autistic Styrofoam.

Petra: Do you mean *artistic* Styrofoam?

Langford da Louse: Yeah, autistic Styrofoam, and I picks up a canna gray spray paint. I tells da checkout guy dat I ain't no graffiti ahtist, dat I'm paintin' some boots wit it. Back at da hideout, I fashion da blocks into boots, I sprays 'em gray, and I straps 'em on da lady's feet. Den I take her to da lake and we gets in a motaboat.

Petra: Okay, you can skip some details. Let's get to the end of the story.

Langford da Louse: Hey, it's my story, lemme finish! I takes her out to da middle a' da lake and I says, "Just in case I'm bein' watched, after I dump youse overboard, pretend dat youse strugglin' and sinkin' for a minute or two. I'll mota back to da shore and leave. I hope youse can swim, but anyway, youse got dem Styrofoam boots to keep youse afloat." So yeah, I didn't bump her off, but I did leave her. I never hoid if she made it or not.

Petra: Well, Langford, I'm seeing you in a different light now. I'm going to ponder this for a few moments.

Langford da Louse: Hey, Saint Petra, while youse is ponderin', may I come troo da gate fer just a small momento to see if any of my friends are heah?

Petra: You mean, just traipse around, taking ganders at all the angels and other Heaven dwellers?

Langford da Louse: Yeah, just like dat.

Petra: Absolutely not. Heaven is a quiet, calm, serene place. Have you heard that rumor on Earth about all the dead rock stars jamming together?

Langford da Louse: Yeah! Right on! I wish I could hear summa dat!

Petra: Well, don't hold your breath. Ha ha, you don't breathe anymore! Excuse me for that joke. But in reality, we don't allow loud noises in Heaven. There is no rock-band-jamming allowed here. Jimi Hendrix doesn't jam with Jim Morrison, but they do play chess together every Thursday morning at ten. Whitney Houston holds a quilting class every Tuesday at two o'clock. Her fellow quilters are Amy Winehouse, Bob Marley, Karen Carpenter, and Frank Sinatra.

Prince holds daily dance and aerobic exercise classes. Everyone is given a bass guitar with a shoulder strap to wear while they work out. They don't have to know how to play, they just pretend. No one actually *needs* to exercise anymore, but it's super-fun to get up and move our spirits with Prince.

Once a month, the *Dead at Twenty-Seven* club meets to discuss the socio-political derivations of a modernistic constitutional exhaustive allocational decline in acquirable shares of blighted pulchritudinous intercontinental ballistic asparagus analysts within an incriminate delectable hypothesis.

Langford da Louse: Sounds tantalizin'. I'll have to drop in and partake of da dashin' discourse.

Petra: Yes. Well, Okay, Langford. Good for you. I hope

you do drop in and partake. Now, to be clear, we *do* allow acoustic music. To that regard, one of our members here in Heaven is so popular that we created a once-a-week event for him.

Langford da Louse: Who's dat? Frank Sinatra?
Petra: Nope.
Langford da Louse: Not Frankie? Okay, Judy Garland?
Petra: Nope.
Langford da Louse: Hmmm, gotta be Elvis.
Petra: Wrong again.
Langford da Louse: Really? I give up.
Petra: Jim Croce, you dunce! Oops. Sorry. But really, you should have known. His songs have the cleverest lyrics. His melodies are brilliant and easy to assimilate. You can't get them out of your head.
Langford da Louse: Ahhh, a' course, ol' Jim Croce! He's Italian, ya know? I love dat one song, "Bad, Bad Leroy Wilson."
Petra: You mean Brown, right? *Brown.*
Langford da Louse: No, I mean—wait a sec—who?
Petra: It's Brown, not Wilson.
Langford da Louse: What? Who's Brown-not-Wilson?
Petra: Not Wilson. *Brown!*
Langford da Louse: Dat's a funny name, Wilson Brown.
Petra: No, no! Oh, just forget it. Let's get back to Mr. Croce. He's so popular up here, and so many spirits attend his concerts, that we feared the clouds wouldn't support everyone gathered so closely together. We created listening pods for groups of no more than six, and the pods are

spaced twenty feet apart. That way we prevent people from falling through.

Langford da Louse: Oh, wow! Dat's awesome!

Petra: I appreciate your enthusiasm, but please refrain from using that *most* overused word. *Fantastic, amazing, lovely, cool,* and *groovy* are acceptable. Even *far out* is admissible. But please, not that A word. Now, who is it that you want to see up here?

Langford da Louse: How about Sal da Slasher.

Petra: Oh, no, definitely not. He didn't even have an interview up here. He went straight *down there* to you-know-where.

Langford da Louse: Okay . . . hmmm. Whaddabout Gretchen da Grabber?

Petra: I remember her. I almost sent her down. She came within an inch of taking the taxi to Toil Foreverville. But I could sense a very slight sweetness behind her cruel facade.

Langford da Louse: So she's heah?

Petra: She's heah—I mean here—but she absolutely cannot have visitors. She's a bad girl, sad girl, lost-everything-she-had girl, livin' in a cloudy pad girl.

Langford da Louse: Oh, darn. Dat Gretchie. I called her Gretchie. She was da best. A real fun gal, ya know what I'm talkin' 'bout?

Petra: Oh, please, of course I know what you're talking about. I wasn't born yesterday. I was born 347 years and sixty-eight days ago. And she wasn't a *real* fun gal. She was a *really* fun gal.

Langford da Louse: Whatevah.

Petra: No! Not *whatever*! If you're going to stay *here* instead of going *down there*, I won't have you perpetrating these word crimes!

Langford da Louse: Well, okey-dokey. I won't say *awes*—I mean da A woid—no more. I mean *any* more! Heyyy. Wait a cat-gone minute. Youse just said, "If you're gonna *stay here* instead of goin' *down there*."

Petra: Oh. I did, didn't I? Oh, darn. Okay, you got me. I can sense that you have a lot of sweetness. You may have led a life of crime, but you aren't a bad person. Dat—I mean *that*—Styrofoam boots story was what tipped the scales in your favor. *It had better be true!*

Langford da Louse: Of course it's true, Saint Petra! It's right dere on youse clipboid, ain't it?

Petra: *Isn't* it. Yes. I was just having a bit of fun with you.

Langford da Louse: Okaaay! Are youse sayin' I'm IN?

Petra Yes, Langford. You're in.

Langford da Louse: Whoopee!!

Petra: Now, Langford, take it easy. Here in Heaven you have to continually prove your worth.

Langford da Louse: Oh, I'll prove my woith, Petra baby! I'll prove it all night! Oh, hey. I can't rememba. Is Brucey Springstone heah or is he still among da livin'?

Petra: It's Springsteen. And no, he's not here yet. We can hardly wait for him, though. I think he and Mr. Croce will get along fine, if they can keep quiet.

Langford da Louse: Yeah, maybe if dey play acoustimatically, they won't be breakin' no rules? I mean, *any* rules!

STORY 7

Petra: Hello there, I can see you peeking over the gate. Please don't be shy.

Arrival: What the... am I really here? I wasn't ready to go. I thought I would have a few more years.

Petra: Considering you *are* here, perhaps it was your time to go. What happened to cause your expiration?

Arrival: I was killed during a disagreement in a bar.

Petra: Well, now, that's not very original. Oh, how I loathe the way people act when under the influence of alcohol. Was it a political discussion? Religious in nature? Or did someone teach you a lesson 'bout messin' with the wife of a jealous man?

Arrival: Nope. I died from being hit over the head with a wine bottle during a disagreement over the pronunciation of Porsche, the automobile.

Petra: Oh, boy. I thought I'd heard everything.

Arrival: As I'm sure you know, it's pronounced *Porsh*-uh, right? The idiot who killed me yelled, "It's *Porsh!*" I yelled back, "*Porsh*-uh!" He punched me on the nose and yelled, "*Porsh!*" I slugged him on the jaw. "*Porsh*-uh!" We kept on for twenty minutes, "Porsh! *Uuugghh!*" "*Porsh*-uh! *Oooof!*" "Porsh! *Thwack!*" "*Porsh*-uh!" Then, *klarnnn!* The last thing I remember was falling to the floor in a shower of chardonnay.

Petra: I'm so angry I can hardly speak. Human interactions have not improved at all in the last five hundred years. Besides, you both are incorrect. The proper pronunciation of Porsche is *Por-skay*.

Arrival: Are you freakin' kiddin' me?!

Petra: I am. I still have no idea how to say it properly. I even contacted the owner of the Porsche car company, and he told me it was top secret and that he couldn't confirm how to say it. But you and your idiot bar friend are typical examples of low forms of humans, and maybe it's best that there is now one fewer low form on the planet. Oh, that wasn't very nice of me to say. Let me ask you, how smart are you when you're not drinking? Wait, that wasn't very nice, either. I don't know what to do with you. I need time to think.

Arrival: Okay. You want me to stand here or what?

Petra: Yes. Just stand there. Get comfortable. Maybe lean against the Gates. It may take an eternity for me to decide what to do with you. And please discontinue that dumb habit of ending a question with "or what?"

STORY 8

Petra: Hello, welcome to Heaven! If you're from the United States, press one to be connected to tech support in India. If you're from India, press two to be connected to tech support in Alabama. Just kidding. As I said, welcome to Heaven. Well, you're not welcome *yet*. But hello, just the same. What's your fable, Mabel?"

Mabel: Oh, wow! It's really *you!* And you knew my name! And you are the legendary Petra, saint of Gate-opening goodness!

Petra: Hello, new arrival. That's quite an opening line. If you're trying to get on my good side, it's working.

Mabel: I'm certainly not trying to get on your bad side. How did you know my name?

Petra: It's all here on the clipboard.

Mabel: Oh. Does it mention that I haven't always been Mabel?

Petra: Let me look. I see it here, yes. You were a man named Crawfarus Broderick Hudson. Your parents couldn't have chosen a more masculine name if they had been held at needlepoint.

Mabel: Right. But ironically, I entered the earthly world with a biological makeup of approximately 35 percent male and 65 percent female. I never felt like a male. All the unpleasant and bad things that I experienced in my life occurred before my transition.

Petra: Well, I do see a lot of sketchy activity here on your data sheet. Some of it can be attributed to ignorance, but as in tax violations, ignorance is no excuse.

Mabel: Sorry, but can you blame me? Speaking of that, may I blame somebody up here for being born in a male body?

Petra: Unfortunately, that window of time has closed. We opened up a period for disgruntled humans to submit claims of imperfection from the year 1742 to last May. You *just* missed it by the hair of your—

Mabel: —chinny-chin-chin?

Petra: Yes! How did you know? Do habitants of Earth still say that?

Mabel: Yes.

Petra: I was saying that in 1689. Who knew that in 2023 humans would still use that silly phrase? Okay, let me see if there is anything of note here. Oh, here's something. Mabel, do you remember the cute little health food stores and the rise in popularity of the bulk food bins back in the 1970s?

Mabel: Yes, I sure do. I worked part-time as a stock boy in a health food store called Sunny's Luscious Goodness during my junior year of high school. I was sixteen. The store manager was a gorgeous, lusty, funny twenty-one-year-old woman named Frolic. I was so energized just being in her presence that I dreamed of sitting up all night with her in bed talking about clothes, hair, the romance novel I was reading, and saying, "Gosh, do you think the TV star Brad Crater is sleeping with his co-star, Misty Streetlamp?"

Petra: Thank you for sharing that, Mabel. Now, about those bulk food bins. I was already up in Heaven by then, but I followed Earth's trends and witnessed their popularity from afar. Most of the early bulk bin items were just regular foods that had been covered in sweet chocolate, a common marketing ploy from way back. Not selling enough bed sheets? Dip 'em in chocolate. Not selling enough bars of soap? Dip 'em in chocolate. Not selling enough sewing machines? Dip 'em in chocolate!

Mabel: You're funny, Saint Petra.

Petra: Thank you, Mabel. Now, do you remember the 1980s?

Mabel: Yes, Saint Petra, I do.

Petra: Formerly seen only at specialty health food stores, bulk bins started appearing in supermarkets and became all the rage in North America. Chocolate-covered almonds, carob peanut clusters, candied ginger chunks, and pretzels dipped in vanilla yogurt. Dried, sugar-coated banana slices and fig-filled cookie bars were sold by the pallet-load every day. Because these items were sold in health food stores and in the health food section of supermarkets, people were duped into thinking they were actually healthy to eat, when in reality these items were just ordinary snacks that had been covered in sugar and fat.

Mabel: I hear you loud and clear, Saint Petra, the all-knowing queen of nutrition.

Petra: Are you still trying to get on my good side?

Mabel: Well, maybe.

Petra: Now we come to the section in your life history where things get interesting.

You were a *nibbler*.

Mabel: I'm not sure what you mean.

Petra: Oh, I'm sure you *do*. It says here that you frequented the bulk bins at your local supermarket three or four times a week but never bought anything. Hmmm. Could it have been because you *nibbled*? There were several signs posted that said "Please Don't Nibble," but we know you ignored them. We also know that you knew it was wrong because you always moved stealthily around the bins, looking left and right before you quietly, quickly lifted a lid. Plus, you would say to yourself, *If you're gonna dip into the bin, might as well take two!* You thought that was funny and clever. Now here you are at the Pearly Gates being judged for your actions. *Now* do you think you were being funny and clever?

Mabel: Well, um . . .

Petra: NO *um*! Just be silent if you want to pause! Never again say *um*

Mabel: Okay, Saint Petra, I won't. Sheesh.

Petra: No, not *sheesh*! Just *no um*! And if you're going to say *sheesh*, you have to say the whole thing: *Sheesh-a-Maria*. Now, if you want to have a chance of staying here instead of going *down there*, tell me how you were able to eat from the bulk bins without buying any of the items, hmmm?

Mabel: All right, Saint Petra. I ni . . . I nib . . . I nibbled! Okay? *I nibbled! I NI-I-I-BU-U-U-LED!*

Petra: That's right, get all that aggression out of you now. I don't want any of that here in Heaven. Speaking of nibbling, how about a band called the Bulk Bin Nibblers. What do you think?

Mabel: It's not bad, Saint Petra.

Petra: Of course it isn't bad. Thank you for admitting that you nibbled. In other words, you *stole* from the market.

Mabel: Yes, I did.

Petra: Yes you did *what?*

Mabel: I st . . . I sto . . . I stole! I *stole! I STOLE!*

Petra: Good for you to admit that. You just stay there in a heap on the cloud floor, sobbing like a baby who has been told it can't have another piece of chocolate-covered broccoli. It's good for you to purge those emotional toxins. I'll wait for you. Okay, that's enough. Let's carry on, my wayward spirit. It says here that you had a meditation practice.

Mabel: Yes. How do you know?

Petra: As you may have heard, God is all-knowing and keeps accurate notes. Now, that isn't true about everything. Realistically, how could God be aware of everything and everybody all the time? But obviously someone from our team was watching you, or at least peeked in on occasion, because it's here on my clipboard.

Mabel: Dang that clipboard!

Petra: I like that you don't use profanity. It's not allowed here in Heaven.

Mabel: I will confess that I once had carnal pleasure at a carnival. In fact, I had carnal pleasure with a carnie at a carnival.

Petra: Hey, is that an original? That's funny!

Mabel: Thank you, Saint Petra! My passionate hobby on Earth was writing jokes and hoping to be discovered as the next great comedian. I never actually tried to get noticed, I just practiced in my bedroom mirror and was bitter about not being famous. I wished that I could have been on TV and played nightclubs. I was secretly envious of any comedian who made it and would disparage them to myself. Part of the problem was being stuck at my job.

I worked as an inspector at a basket factory. After the weavers were finished, I looked over every basket for imperfections before passing them on to the workers who sprayed them with fire-proofing poison. Then the baskets got boxed and shipped off to retail stores, where consumers bought them as frivolous knick-knacks and set them on shelves and put junk in them. Eventually, they ended up in thrift stores and yard sales, then ultimately in the city dump. So you can see, I couldn't try to attain my dream of being a comedian when I was needed as a basket inspector.

Petra: You know, Mabel, I think you could have succeeded if you had tried. Have you heard that cool song by Bachman-Turner Overdrive called "Average Man"? It has the lyric, "They're wishing, not working, and that's not the way. For what comes too easy is thrown away."

Mabel: I don't know that song, but thanks for that, Saint Petra. It's poignant and apropos.

Petra: Hey, cool name for a folk music duo: Poignant and Apropos.

Mabel: You're a funny daughter of a sea biscuit, Saint Petra!

Petra: Hey, now, don't get too chummy. I might be sending you *down there*.

Mabel: All right. Now I must tell you that my passionate hobby was entertaining people by making balloon figures.

Petra: Oh, that's marvelous! Please show me—oops, I forgot we have no balloons here in heaven.

Mabel: Dang it.

Petra: Wait. You can use whisps of cloud material! Go ahead and try it.

Mabel: Okay. (She reaches down, grabs a batch of cloud, and begins working it with her hands.)

Petra: Wow, I can see that you're making a horse!

Mabel: No, Saint Petra, it's a frog riding a bicycle.

Petra: Oops. Sorry. But hey, it has to be hard adjusting to working with a new medium, right?

Mabel: Yes. But I'll get better if I can practice.

Petra: Maybe we'll lighten up your daily chores so that you can keep working on your cloud formations.

Mabel: Wait—we have to *work* here in Heaven?

Petra: Yes. Everyone has to continue making a contribution to society, even here in Heaven.

Mabel: Fair enough. Could comic performances be my contribution?

Petra: Sure, but you'll also have regular chores, like sweeping the sidewalk and trimming the clouds in your neighborhood. Did you know that clouds grow and have to be trimmed?

Mabel: I really don't know clouds at all. Which side of the clouds would I have to trim, the yard side or the street side?

Petra: Both sides now.

Mabel: Okay, well, if I'm allowed to stay here in Heaven, I'll gladly sweep the sidewalks and trim the clouds on my street. Which day is the garbage picked up?

Petra: We don't have garbage pickup days because we don't generate any trash. You'll be sweeping up wisps of clouds and trimming hedges and shrubbery that are made of heavy concentrations of condensation. The cloud remnants simply evaporate into the air. When you've finished your chores, you can perform in the neighborhood square.

Mabel: I wonder if anyone will like my routines.

Petra: Oh, I think you'll have fans here.

Mabel: That's all good to know, Saint Petra. On another note, I'm curious about a rumor that is circulating back on Earth that says divorced parents reunite in Heaven. My parents divorced when I was eight years old. Will they be reunited here in Heaven?

Petra: It depends. Parents who remarried do not reunite with their original spouses, they reunite with the spouse they were married to at the time of their death. If neither parent remarries, then yes, they are reunited. If only one parent remarries and the other does not, the two are given a two-hour coffee-and-conversation session every other Saturday with each other. The remarried parent's most recent spouse is encouraged, but not required, to attend the session.

Mabel: May I ask another question?

Petra: Just as long as you don't *axe* me a question.

Mabel: Funny, Saint Petra. We know that dried apples are called *dried apples*, dried peaches are called *dried peaches*, and dried apricots are called *dried apricots*. Why then, are dried plums called *prunes*?

Petra: People expect me to know everything! Now, let's finish up this interview, shall we? It says here that you habitually put broccoli stems, celery, chicken bones, and peach pits down your garbage disposal. That was a dumb-dumb thing to do. And you wondered why the disposal often got stuck and your sink drain clogged! Sheesh-a-Maria, Mabel!

Mabel: Sorry, Saint Petra. I told you I did a lot of dumb things before transitioning to a woman.

Petra: No excuse! Let's see . . . what else? Okay, here. You thought it was cool to pretend you were a big-rig trucker with your cute little diesel engine pickup truck, letting the engine idle every time you parked instead of shutting it off. It was not necessary and did nothing but waste fuel and annoy people.

Mabel: Oh, sorry, I thought it was best to never shut off a diesel engine.

Petra: That notion was created by the DFSC (Diesel Fuel Sellers Cooperative) and the DEMA (Diesel Engine Manufacturers Association) to sell more fuel and engine parts, and it wasn't true. Also, you didn't need to avoid eating egg yolks. You could have eaten them with no negative effects on your health. You either threw away or fed to your dog 12,183 egg yolks during your lifetime, all of them full of yummy golden goodness. Shame on you. Think of all the cute little chicken butts that squeezed out an egg for you *twelve thousand one hundred eighty-three times*! During the years that you didn't have a dog, you simply dropped those yolks carelessly into your garbage disposal. Sheesh-a-Marie, Mabel!

Mabel: Now that you put it that way, I am indeed ashamed.

Petra: Good. I mean, I'm glad you are feeling some remorse. By the way, we know that you put gum and boogers under your desk in grammar school.

Mabel: Uh-oh.

Petra: And yes, it counts against you. Now, give me a few minutes to digest and assimilate all the historical data on you.

Mabel: Go easy on me, please!

Petra: Don't be so desperate. It's unflattering.

Mabel: Sorry.

Petra: What, are you Canadian? Please stop saying sorry. To be clear, I love Canadians, but *sorry* flows out of their mouths like foggy breath on a January morning.
Mabel: Saint Petra! That's a perfect title for a movie or a book!
Petra: What?
Mabel: Foggy Breath on a January Morning.
Petra: No, Mabel. *Band name!*

✳ ✳ ✳

So there you have it, folks. This is what life is like as a gatekeeper in Heaven. Are you sure you want to come? There's a raging party *down there*, you know.

QUIT HONKING!
(I'M PEDALING AS FAST AS I CAN)

Yesterday I applied for a job that I knew I was fully qualified for. I was giddy with the sense that I would soon be chosen as the best out of all the applicants. I could feel a pleasant pang in my left middle toe telling me so. (And you thought pangs were only in your stomach; so did I!) Those clever pangs in my toe also tell me when it's going to rain. (Speaking of astronauts, do they feel a pang in their fangs when they drink Tang? Are you old enough to remember Tang, that American powdered-drink mix brand that NASA sent on John Glenn's Mercury flight in February 1962? I am. I drank it as a child, and look how wonderfully I turned out.)

There I sat in a cheap, flimsy plastic folding chair in the back row of a somewhat-descript office that was painted with Sherman-Williams *Baby Butt Breeze* yellow. The office had short-pile blue-and-orange-speckled carpeting and featured tinted glass windows. On the west wall was a Bryant T6-PAC01-A thermostat, which regulated the operation of a Bryant 926S060 gas furnace and a Bryant 126CNA048 air conditioner, keeping the space at a pleasant temperature. The eight other applicants were chatting among themselves, but I wanted to conserve my energy and focus on obtaining this job. I kept quiet and didn't converse or even smile at the other hopeful candidates. That was my plan, to psyche out my competition by being detached, cool, and aloof.

Soon, a tall, fit, wide-hipped woman entered. She had gray hair and a thin, Spanish-looking face. She extruded—I mean *exuded*—a lovely energy and smiled as she spoke. "Hello, my name is Nazus Azareb. Who here wants to be a cactus whisperer?"

I remained motionless as I watched eight arms quickly shoot up into the air. Nazus looked directly at me, grinned, and asked, "Don't you? What's your name?"

"Goud. Goud Sugref."

"Now, Goud, don't *you* want to be a cactus whisperer for us?"

I couldn't stay aloof while looking into Miss Azareb's lovely eyes. "Actually, yes, I do!" I blurted, then let loose with a wide smile.

"Okay, then!" Nazus said as she turned back to the assembled group.

"Here at Azareb Cactus Auto Parts, we infuse love and life-affirming encouragement into every piston, camshaft, water pump, and fan belt. All of our auto parts are made from the flesh of cactus plants. My father, Cire Azareb, invented and perfected the manufacturing technique.

"The auto parts industry has been using metal and

plastic for far too long. We introduced the world's first automatic transmission impeller made from *Melocactus lemairei*. Soon we were turning out many different parts. They have proven to be as reliable or more so than metal or plastic. Here's our secret. We *nurture* our plants, from the moment a cactus shoot punctures the soil until it's harvest time.

"Your job will be to walk the cactus fields every day and speak words of encouragement to the crops. You'll also lovingly, carefully caress the plants so that they grow healthy and strong."

"Really?" I said. "We caress their cute little arms and bodies and speak to them?"

"Yes!" Nazus said. "Plants can hear us. You'll be required to say things like, 'You are strong and beautiful, but don't dwell on your physical gifts because you are as smart as you are pretty.'"

"Weird and cool," I said. "What if I said to a plant, 'Your mama is an oil pan on a Cadillac and your daddy is a Ferrari radiator.'"

Miss Azareb chuckled. "I think you might hear the plant reply, 'Goud, I think you have a few loose lug nuts.'"

Miss Azareb handed a job application to all nine of us and strolled about the room as we filled in the blanks. She happened to amble by as I was circling the number twelve in the section Circle Highest Level of Education. She looked at my application and remarked, "Oh. I . . . I didn't realize."

I turned to look her in the eye. "What? What didn't you realize?"

"That twelve is the highest grade you've completed." Suddenly flustered and desperate to stay in the running for this job, I scrambled to improvise an explanation. "Oh . . . uh, that's the highest level of *high school* that I completed." I grinned awkwardly. "It's certainly not the total number of *all* my years of education."

Nazus smiled and curtly said, "If that's true, please circle the number sixteen for *total* number of years." Now her voice had a tone of condescension. "And write the name of the college that you attended." She swished away and continued meandering about the room.

I made a quick scan of the other applicants. Could they all be college graduates? My confidence sank. I didn't want to lose this job on a simple and silly technicality. Did I go to college or not? I knew I shouldn't lie, but I felt I had gained the knowledge and life experience in my thirty-eight years on the planet equal to that of any four-year diploma. As I thought about it, I got a twinge of anger. I narrowed my eyelids and pursed my lips. I recalled my last date with a woman who told me, as she dropped me off at the bus station, "You're fit, funny, worldly, and wise, and I'm sure you'll find your way in the world. But I simply can't be with a man who doesn't have a degree." She then laughed as she pressed on the accelerator pedal and called out, "Good luck earning your bachelor's in being a bachelor!"

My anger turned to boldness as I circled "16." In the space for Name of School, I wrote "College of Life."

* * *

I was sifting turds out of my roommate's cat box when the call came. It was from Azareb Cactus Auto Parts. (I had wisely entered the name and number into my phone contacts.) I playfully chirped, "Hello, is this Azareb Cactus Auto Parts?"

"Yes, it is. I'm Nazus Azareb. Is Goud Sugref there?"

"Oh, hi, Miss Azareb!" I said a bit too enthusiastically.

"Hello, Goud. I'd like to talk to you about your job application. We liked you, but we simply can't hire you without a college degree." My enthusiasm quickly dissipated. "We thought it was clever of you to circle '16' and write 'College of Life' as the name of your school, but we won't be able to bring you on board. Sorry."

I blurted, "But wait! Can we talk about it? I'm certain that I would make a great cactus whisperer! The best!"

"You probably would be a fine whisperer, Goud, but we have a firm policy of hiring only college graduates."

I pleaded, "But Miss Azareb, at the college of life, we never really graduate, yet we never cease to educate."

"I'm sorry, Goud."

I adopted a pleasant tone. "Now, Nazus—may I call you Nazus?"

"Let's keep it professional. Please call me Miss Azareb."

"Okay, Miss Azareb. I know I have a lack of credits, but the lessons I've learned on the street have kept me alive and on my feet." I could sense, even over the phone, that she was shaking her head. "How about the fact that my resume is a mile long! My mind and my back are both strong." Silence. I could tell she didn't care or understand.

I was losing steam, succumbing to the loss of the job of my dreams.

"Can you suggest where I might apply for a job, since you won't bend the rules?" She softly mumbled something. I asked, "Excuse me, what did you say?"

In a detached monotone she said, "Why don't you go back to school?"

I was shocked. I thought I had made a sort of spiritual connection with her. I felt we were kindred souls. I suddenly realized that I needed to let her go from my life, but I didn't want to rudely hang up. I didn't want her to feel bad about her decision to not hire me. I wanted her to remember me fondly. With a sweet lilt in my voice I said, "I hear you saying to me that I would make a wonderful cactus whisperer if only I had a college degree."

She responded softly, "Yes."

"I hear you saying to me that I should consider going back to school."

"That's right, Goud."

"I'll consider it, Miss Azareb. Thank you. Goodbye." I pressed the circular red button on my phone to end the call and contemplated the next phase of my life.

Now that being a professional cactus whisperer was off the table, what to do? What to do? For now, I'll keep collecting my unemployment checks and food stamps, sitting for hours at Wasting the Day Away but Making Real Human Connections, So Don't Knock Me! Coffee, Tacos, and Frozen Custard. I'll hold a copy of *War and Peace*, pretending to read it. I want to look interesting to customers as they come and go. I'll look up and slightly smile at them all, hoping to provoke a connection that could ultimately lead to a gainful situation of some sort. (If you visit this coffee shop, won't you please come up and introduce yourself to me? I promise to give you scattered attention and make eye contact with one eye while I scan the room with my other eye for people who may have more to offer.)

To put my College of Life degree to good use, I spent some of my time composing this soulful song:

QUIT HONKING!

Here I am only trying to make my way in this world.
Thrown out on the road of life, dodging the cars like a squirrel.
Is it just me, or do you feel it too, that the world is turning faster?
Hey! Quit honking! I'm pedaling as fast as I can!
Walking down the street, I am repeatedly nipped at the heels.
Quickening my step is fruitless because under my feet are banana peels.
Haven't you heard, this new fast pace of life is really not so good!
Hey! Quit honking! I'm pedaling as fast as I can!
Strolling through the park, I encounter an old high school buddy.
He's intense. He brags that he's doing great. He says to me, "What are you up to?"

I can't be outdone and say, "I married a fashion model, we live in Paris, and I own a fleet of Hummers." Hey! Quit honking! I'm pedaling as fast as I can!

(Please go to your favorite music streaming platform and listen to the song "Quit Honking!" by Lucky Doug Fergus. Thank you!)

BEDROOM REMODELS

Ralph was a retired air force jet engine mechanic. He had joined the USAF when he was only seventeen and so, after the minimum time of twenty years, was able to retire as a spry, eager thirty-seven-year-old. Soon Ralph became bored, however, and at his wife's urging, he got a job at a home appliance and hardware superstore, Crap for My House.

After working there for several months, Ralph noticed that many contractors did kitchen and bathroom remodel work, but no one was doing bedroom remodels. He was certain that he could fill a need and make a killing in this neglected market. With joy in his heart and a spring in his step, he gave notice to quit his job at Crap for My House. On his last day at work, he told several coworkers of his brilliant plan. "I'm going to capitalize on what absolutely, most assuredly is going to be the next major housing trend: *bedroom* remodels!" His coworkers stared at him blankly. "You all should seriously consider quitting and joining me in my new company!" They all wished him well and said goodbye.

Ralph's sister-in-law built a gorgeous, easy-to-navigate website for his new company and set up an easy credit card payment system. But as the days crawled by, no one clicked the Contact button. He spent $3,000 for five thousand business cards (that had an incorrect phone number because he was too eager to get them printed and didn't proofread them first), five hundred hats, and five hundred lousy, thin T-shirts with the company logo that peeled off the first time they got washed. He took out a home equity line of credit to purchase a beautiful, contractor-outfitted, $89,000 work truck. In six months it was repossessed for failure to make payments.

One day Ralph was handing out business cards (this time with the corrected phone number handwritten on the back and SEE BACK OF CARD scribbled in the front) in the parking lot of a sports bar.

A woman approached him, looked at the peeling letters on his company T-shirt, stared at the business card he held up to her face and said, "Bedroom remodels, huh?" Ralph smiled broadly, revealing his lovely coffee-tobacco- and Pepsi-colored teeth.

"That's correct, ma'am! We're the best!"

"Uh ... okay. But aren't bedrooms just four walls?"

Ralph stumbled. "Um, no. Uh, well ... technically, yes, but—but it's an art form to get a bedroom just right. We have designers that will give you whatever you want in your bedroom."

The woman burst out laughing, turned, and walked away as she said, "I don't need your designers to give me what I want in my bedroom, honey. I got my husband for that!"

Ralph is now back at Crap for My House, where he works five days a week advising people on the difference between string and twine. Most of his pay goes toward the loan he took out on two enormous custom-made neon signs that he had purchased for his rented building. They are so pretty, bright, colorful, and cheerful that he couldn't stand to get rid of them. His only real problem now is when the neighbors complain that they can't sleep at night because of the brightly flashing RALPH'S RUMPUS ROOM REMODELS signs that he installed on the roof of his house.

COOKIES FOR CORKYLEE

Every morning I wrote out a list of the many items that needed my attention. Anything that wasn't completed during the day had to be added on to the next day's list. Here is a small, partial list from yesterday:

- Clip toenails.
- Finish blueberry granola before opening the new box of cranberry granola.
- Brush teeth. Use the new tube of Tom's of Maine Apricot/Tuna flavor.
- Listen to Spanish lesson while sitting on the pot.
- Write 200-page thesis on the hypothetical alignment of conjectural hunches.
- Return the too-small red corduroy pants to Josie.
- Create a company that manufactures steam-operated sawmill equipment, mining machinery, boilers, pumps, crushers, pulverizers, and other rock and cement milling stuff.

- Pull weeds in the 8' x 4' flower bed on the east side of house.

In trying to accomplish as many list items as possible in one day, I was making myself wobbly, glassy-eyed, and qualmish.

One morning, while I was eating a bowl of cherries (I was eating the bowl, not the cherries), I read an Instagram post by a nineteen-year-old ectomorphic weight-lifting-instructor-diet-and-nutrition-expert-lifestyle-coach-supermarket checker. She suggested I throw away my microtask-accomplishing timeline and instead write in large letters on a blank 8' x 11' sheet: BREATHE. But getting rid of my detailed list created even *more* anxiety. (*Anxiety* is a funny word. I wonder if it was created out of the words *angst* and *society*?)

Back to my problem/issue (*prissue*?) with anxiety.

I had purchased several self-help books to ease my apprehension about time management. I intended to read them rapidly so that I could fix myself in months, not years. But with each new purchase, I would set the book on my bedside table, never to pop the cover. The pile grew so high that I had to have the bedroom ceiling raised from eight to twelve feet.

Speaking of self-help, I had spent the night in a San Diego jail in 1987 when I was caught walking out of a bookstore with a copy of *It's Easier to Tell You How to Live Than to Do It Myself* without paying. I finally convinced the three policemen at the station—Gordon, Andy, and Stewart—to let me go by explaining that I assumed the self-help section of the store was the same as a Help Yourself section.

My next plan to be more efficient with my time was to attend self-help seminars. The act of experiencing a dynamic, attractive, zestful speaker in person was sure to make a much greater impact on me than simply reading printed words on a page.

Serendipitously, an email arrived in my inbox: *Goud Sugref, you won't want to miss Piss Pot Poor No More!* It announced an upcoming human development and financial enrichment seminar. Hmmm, interesting. I reckoned that I could use that information in all areas of my life. I immediately clicked the SUCKERS CLICK HERE button. *The biggest secret to gaining wealth is having the social skills to interact positively with all types of people.* I have always thought that I was a fairly easygoing person and blended well with people of different races and nationalities, but maybe I could learn a new trick or two. And I'm not poor by any means, but who wouldn't like to be more financially abundant? I decided to go.

I was riddled with apprehension about attending the seminar alone, so I invited my friend CorkyLee. I told her that I would happily pay the reasonable $178 attendance fee to have her come along and give me emotional support. I was sure that this weekend retreat would be the key that would unlock the titanium vault door that trapped my mental and financial freedom. I gladly sold all fourteen of my prized original, still-in-the-box 1960s Hasbro GI Joe dolls stored in my attic, along with my complete collection of sixty-five never-before-played

1980s Richard Simmons's Sweatin' to the Oldies aerobics VHS tapes to produce the $356 needed for the two symposium tickets.

On the appointed date, I picked up CorkyLee in front of her apartment. We immediately began a weighty conversation centered on nuclear-socio-political themes.

"Hi, CorkyLee, how are you today?" I asked.

"Fine, Goud," she said.

"That's nice," I replied.

She asked, "How are *you* today?"

"Oh, fine," I answered. After that rousing exchange, we sat in silence for a quarter of the hour-long drive to the airport.

I was giving an acceptance speech in front of five thousand people, for having been voted the best hotel maintenance person in America for the sixth year in a row, when CorkyLee rudely alarmed me out of my daydream. "Hey, Goud. Sorry, but I need you to take the next exit and stop at a gas station minimart."

I tried to not let it bother me. "It's only forty-five minutes to the airport. Can it wait?"

"Sorry, no."

I assumed she needed to evacuate something, so I didn't ask the reason for the urgent need to visit a minimart. "I see several businesses up ahead at that interchange." CorkyLee grinned. I veered off the highway and parked in front of the Pump & Munch gas and mini market as she hopped out. "I'll be quick!"

Four minutes later she came striding back to the car with a cup of coffee and a small item in a wrapper.

Settling back into the passenger seat, she exhaled. "Well, that's better!"

"You really had to go, huh?"

She shook her head and said no.

I didn't want to pry, but since we were about to spend three days in a human development seminar I didn't want to walk on eggshells, either.

"What's in the package?"

"Oh, this?" She held up what looked like some sort of food item. "I'm not ashamed to admit that I have an addiction to these things." I didn't recognize the product. She blurted, "It's a Lenny and Larry's protein cookie. They are the *best!* You haven't had them yet? Oh man! They're sweeping the nation. Only the *best* stores carry them."

"Well then, I'm missing out. What do they taste like?"

"Healthy, yummy, soft, heavenly, and packed with pro-teeny. I need to have at least three a day. Sometimes I have six. That's why I have to stop often when I travel. It works best if we can time it so that when we stop to get gas, I get a cookie."

I asked, "You couldn't go the one hour from your home to the airport without a cookie?"

"No! I hadn't had one yet today! I wasn't sure if the airport snack shop would carry them, so I panicked. They're not in every store yet. Only the best—"

"—stores carry them. I heard you, I heard you!"

I waited for her to offer me a bite. As she nibbled away at the cookie, I kept an eye on it. When it was almost gone I asked, "Hey, can I have a little taste?"

"No!" she blurted. "Every Lenny and Larry's is *precious.*

It's as if they make them just for *me*. Once I open the package, I have to eat all of it myself. The next time we stop, you can go in and get one for yourself. *If* the store carries them, that is. They're not in—"

"—every store yet!" CorkyLee grinned as we said in unison, "Only the best stores carry them!"

"Also," she said, "I need to have a cup of coffee when I eat them. I have to have a small bite and a small sip of coffee in my mouth at the same time. I slowly and gently mash the mixture in my mouth, like a mama bird masticating seeds and bugs for her babies. It takes me about twenty minutes to eat one. I savor the flavor slowly, like a fine, coffee-and-cookie-flavored wine that can't be consumed before its time."

I rolled my eyes without turning my head so that CorkyLee couldn't see me. Oh boy, it looked like I was going to spend a few days with a fruitcake. I thought I knew her fairly well; obviously, I didn't.

We backed out of the parking space and returned to the highway. CorkyLee said, "Lenny and Larry's comes in several flavors. Each time I buy one, I choose a different flavor."

I inquired, "Why don't you buy them by the box or the case?"

"No! I can't!" she cried. "I'd eat them all at one sitting! I have to buy only one at a time."

"I see."

Arriving at the airport, we left the car in long-term parking and hustled into the terminal building. We were close to being late and had to rush through security and then find our gate. We were still on time. We sat in the last two available chairs in the boarding area.

CorkyLee began looking at her phone, swiping up slowly. After three minutes she dropped the phone in her lap, turned to me with a dead-serious face, and said, "I can't go."

I was dumbstruck. "What? Why?! You're kidding, aren't you?"

"No, Goud! I really can't go. I was reading about my favorite bass player in my favorite band, Grand Turner Overfunk. See?" She showed me an article on her phone.

"It says that Fredmel Schachurner developed a fear of flying. I worship him! I've spent hundreds of hours studying his playing style."

I was intrigued at hearing this from CorkyLee. "I had no idea you played bass, CorkyLee!"

She replied, "I don't, but I've spent hundreds of hours studying marvelous Fredmel Schachurner's bass lines and technique. And if *he* has a fear of flying, *I* can't possibly fly, don't you see?"

I turned my head and rolled my eyes. CorkyLee threw up her hands. "Well, it's settled. We're going to have to drive to the seminar."

I stood up. "This whole weekend was *my* idea! I invited *you*! And now *you're* making the rules?"

"Sorry, Goud. But if you want me to go, I simply *can't* fly."

I sat down and scratched my chin. "Okay, here's what we'll do. I'll get on the plane. You take the car and drive to the event."

She softened and flashed her eyes in an adorably androgynous way. "Um, Goud? My pal, my buddy? I don't have a driver's license." Incredulous, I asked why not. "Years ago I stopped driving, sold my car, and cut my license in half to protest the fact that vinyl is used in most car seats. Vinyl is on the engendered species list. Didn't you know that?"

I started to smile but stopped, turned my head, and asked, "Don't you mean *endangered* species list?"

She snapped, "No! I meant what I said! It's not right! They can't make more vinyl, right?! As we speak, they are mining the bottom of the ocean for the raw materials to make vinyl. Once that raw material has been completely removed from all sea floors, all the bees in the world will die."

I stood up again. "Okay. Here's what we're gonna do. We toss these plane tickets in the trash, drive the one hour back to my house, and pick up two sleeping bags from the camping gear in my garage. Then we drive the six hours to the event. We'll get there late and sleep in the back of the truck."

CorkyLee grinned ear to ear. "Great! Call the organizers now. Cancel that cabin rental you paid for and get your money back, since we'll be slumbering in the truck."

"Hey, smarty pants. Good idea. I like your thinkin', Lincoln."

She chuckled. "And maybe figure on a little more than six hours for my—I mean *our*—Lenny and Larry's cookies-and-coffee stops."

※ ※ ※

"Hey Goud, just letting you know, if you get tired, I can take over driving duties."

I said, "But you said you don't have a driver's license."

CorkyLee responded, "License, schmicense. My dad was a professional motorcycle racer and taught me to drive when I was ten."

"Just because he was a motorcycle racer didn't automatically make him an expert driver and teacher."

"Well, yes it did, obviously! Think about it. One machine has two extra wheels, but the concept is the same."

I shook my head and chortled. "Really? You think the concept is the same?"

CorkyLee rolled her eyes and laughed out loud. "Obviously, silly!"

"It just *might* be against the law for you to drive on a public road with no license."

"Yes, but I'm actually a really good driver."

"By the way, is it a *driver's* license or a *driver* license?"

"Good question, and here is your answer. A *driver's* license is one type of license for many drivers. A *driver* license is one license for one driver."

I replied, "Hmmm, interesting. So then, would a very small license for the purpose of operating a motor vehicle be called a *Minnie Driver license?*"

CorkyLee busted out a giggle, then displayed her beautiful, smiling face. "She's my favorite actress of all time!"

I said, "I thought your favorite actress might be Wynona Ryder because of your dad, You know, *rider*?"

"Aww, Goud, that was clever. Like you!" She flashed that wonderful beaming face again. I didn't know how to respond to compliments, so I just smiled back. Maybe this seminar would teach me to appreciate someone saying they admired one of my traits.

CorkyLee was a friend of a friend, not really a friend of mine. I had met her on several occasions, but we had never spent more than a few minutes chatting. Even though she was turning out to be the aforementioned fruitcake, I wondered if she would become more than a friend. Miserable me; I was a terrible loner. I was always open to having a romantic partner, but on dating someone new, I would look for flaws until I found a reason to break up. I never explored the good qualities in a person.

Now, on our way to the seminar, I figured it was time to be open to the good parts of a human. Instead of looking at CorkyLee as strange, weird, or repugnant, I saw her as capricious, whimsical, enthralling, and other names of amusement park costumed characters. I was already floating on the high of the maybe that CorkyLee could be my new mate.

* * *

As we boogied along the highways and byways through the night, I kept awake by pretending that I was Rob Mac-Cachren leading the Baja 1000 off-road race. "Hey, watch it there, Speed Racer!" CorkyLee yelled out. "Who do you think you are, Sammy Hagar? You can't drive fifty-five?"

"Oops, sorry! I was leading a race in Mexico in my mind."

CorkyLee rolled her eyes and shook her head. "Oh, Goud."

Twenty minutes of silence later, she suddenly said, "I'm strongly considering becoming a public figure and an online fitness coach. Should I get my teeth whitened first or get fake boobs?"

"First," I said, "you'll have to work out a lot and eat very little so that you are in a constant state of calorie deficit. One must be able to bounce a quarter off your tummy and rump."

"*Who* will need to bounce a quarter off my tummy or rump?"

"Well, gosh, *anyone*! If you want, I'll do it!"

She became agitated. "Actually, I would prefer that no one bounced anything off my tummy or rump."

"Okay. No bouncing anything off any part of you. To be a top fitness coach, you might want to have a baby. Then you can slim down and tighten up to demonstrate that anyone can be a foxy mommy. You can also demonstrate workouts while carrying your child. It's the latest thing on Instagram."

"Right! Then I could say I'm a mother, and look at my flat tummy! If I can do it, so can you! Follow me for tips and tricks!"

"Now you're thinkin'," I said. "You can proclaim that you're balancing your extraordinarily important and busy mothering duties with your immensely meaningful and hectic married life. You'll show that your life is as full and frenzied as a one-legged woman in an ass-kicking contest!"

"That's right, and I'll show them that my life is as frantic as a one-armed paper hanger, but look at me! Here I am, doing it all!"

I burst out, "Oh, CorkyLee, you're going to be an Instagram star and maybe even cross over to YouTube!"

She said, "This is all fascinating, but what about people who can't have kids, like me?"

I was taken by surprise and was a hundredth of a second away from thoughtlessly asking, *What's wrong with you? Why can't you have kids?* when I slammed the brakes on my vocal cords. Phew! I dodged an awkward and uncomfortable situation. Oh, sheesh. I'm still a big dork, even though I think I'm evolving. I hope I didn't say too much about the whole Instagram fitness trainer idea. Maybe I offended her. Dang it! But she didn't seem bothered by the discussion.

I asked, "Don't online fitness instructors have to be experts at working out?"

"Oh, no. They just have to be thin, have a booty that sticks way out, and say things like, 'One more! Let's get serious! You're lookin' good!' Oh, and it helps if you admit that you have a major flaw or personal problem. You want to play up the emotionally vulnerable factor. That really brings in the clients. You don't want to appear too perfect."

I asked, "So . . . do *you* work out?"

She answered, "Um, well, not really, not yet. But I'm genetically lean, so I can say I got this body from years of HIIT."

"What's HIIT?"

"It means high intensity interval training."

I said, "I gather you haven't actually tried this high intensity interval training yet."

"Right. I have not. But I can talk about it like a boss! I've studied Mr. Yates's training principles. He's the guy who told me about it."

"Now, Corkmeister. Do you mind if I call you Corkmeister?"

"Please don't! Yuck, that's just... no."

"All right then, but getting back to your original question of teeth or boobs, let me see your chompers." She flashed her fangs. "Teeth are great. Get the boobs—if you must. But I don't think you should. From what I see on Instagram, *small* is in."

CorkyLee grinned. "Oh Goud, you know how to make a person feel good. Hey! It's time for another Lenny and Larry's cookie-and-coffee stop."

"Really? Again?"

"Yes, I told you I'm addicted to them."

I chuckled and shook my head. "I suppose there are worse things to which you could be addicted."

"Right! Alcohol or drugs can getcha messed up!"

"No, I mean addicted to other foods, such as... oh, I don't know... pickled snail testicles."

CorkyLee laughed and bounced up and down in her seat. "Oh man! Right?! My favorite meal is a pickled snail testicles sandwich on toasted Ezekiel bread with honey mustard and cherry jelly!"

※ ※ ※

The hum of my truck tires on the highway was hypnotizing me to sleep as we rolled along down the road. The rock-and-roll radio station wasn't keeping me awake because it was playing the same old, boring thirty-five songs that we hear on every radio station across North America. These same songs have been playing on every rock station for fifty years. Never do we hear any songs by other musicians, as if some kind of rock-and-roll radio mafia controls the airplay of all rock music. I suspect that this corrupt, immoral group demands that only these thirty-five songs—*and no others*—are allowed to be played or else people will mysteriously disappear, only to be found years later on the bottom of a lake, their arms and legs bound with eight-track cassette tape.

"Hey, Goud," CorkyLee said, "I've been thinking about a heap of things lately. May I throw some thoughts out and get your opin?"

"Sure, Cork. Do you mind if I call you Cork?"

"Nope, that's cool. So, here's one of my thoughts: when does a seed become a pit?" I shook my head and shrugged my shoulders.

I said, "I wonder if the poor condition of many of our nation's roads and highways could be fixed by paving them with olive pits. Actually, I've thought about using avocado pits instead of olive pits. They're bigger, it would take fewer of them, and the road would be bumpier for better grip on the tires."

CorkyLee approved. "Ooh, I like that idea!"

I asked, "What about peach pits? If we used them as paving stones, they would allow rainwater to penetrate the road because they have those little holes."

She replied, "Right! And it's fun to say fast: peach pit peach pit peach pit. Surely there's a rap group called Peach Pit, right? I'll look on Spotify . . . ha! There *is* a group called Peach Pit! But of *course* there is, right? As Douglas Fergus wrote in his first book, *Small Portions Café*, just when you think all band names have been taken, they have been—or soon will be! It was only a matter of time before a band called itself Peach Pit. Curiously, the real Peach Pit is not a rap group but kind of a folkie/soft rock group."

I said, "If it were a rap group, it would be spelled Peech Pyt, right, Cork?" She chuckled softly.

We were rolling up the highway, enjoying a few precious moments of silence, when CorkyLee piped up, "Hey, Goud, remember when we left the last gas-and-cookie stop? The clerk said *drive safe*. I think he meant drive *safely*, right?"

I thought for a moment. "I believe you are correct, CorkyLee. I believe the proper use of that salutation is drive *safely*. Drive *safe*, on the other hand, would be how you'd describe a person driving a box made for holding valuables that had tires and a steering wheel installed. Then one could say, 'Have a nice day! Drive *safe*!'"

"I think you'd actually say, 'Have a nice day! Drive *your* safe!' Or 'Have fun driving your safe!'"

After this rousing conversation, another ten-minute stretch of silence went by. Then CorkyLee suddenly punctured it. "Hey, Mr. Truck Driver! Should we start a company that creates a line of automotive products, like fruit-flavored windshield washer fluid? Or liquid fragrances that you drop in your gas tank to produce a lovely exhaust aroma, like, oh . . . I'm thinking vanilla/cinnamon?"

"Sure, Cork! Because what the world needs now, more than love, sweet love, is another line of frivolous products that require plastic containers that will end up in a whale's tummy!"

"Oh, come on, Goudie-the-wet-blanket, master of doom and gloom. Okay, well, do you like puffed snacks? I think we could puff just about anything and it would sell. For the most part, humans will eat anything that's light and puffy and crunchy. You could have puffed liver nuggets, puffed socks, puffed golf balls, and puffed lima beans."

"Let's think about it! If we think long and hard about it, maybe *we'll* become puffed ourselves!"

Another five minutes of pleasant silence ensued, then "Hey, Goudie, do you think that truckers have big-rig envy, as if it's cooler and more macho to drive trucks that haul things, like giant earth-moving machines or enormous industrial air-conditioning-system parts?"

"Yes, CorkyLee, I think they do. Imagine a macho truck driver stopping at a truck stop and chatting with other drivers, then having to admit that he hauled pillows, kittycat vests, vegetarian jerky, and knitting yarn!"

"Oh, Goudie, you make me laugh, you silly duck!"

"Hey, you know those wire twist-tie thingies we use to close the tops of plastic bags or a bunch of kale or cords?"

I asked. "If all's right with the universe, they should be twisted closed *clockwise*, right? But often when I buy a product that has one of those thingies, it's twisted closed *counter*clockwise! Can you believe it?"

"OMG, Goudie, baby! That's just wrong! They should always, *always* be twisted closed clockwise and opened counterclockwise! I wonder if some of those products come from another country, like England or Australia, and they tighten those twist-tie thingies by turning them counterclockwise, which is *so weird and wrong* to us but is *normal* for them!"

"Oh, gosh, Cork! I think you've hit upon the answer! I bet that's the very reason! Oh, CorkyLee, you're a smarty pantaloon!"

* * *

We had been on the road for hours now, but we were nowhere close to exhausting interesting things to talk about.

"Goudie, I think I'm falling in like with you."

I grinned at her and let that statement sit there in the air for a while. I was falling in like with her, too, but I wasn't sure when—or if—I should be demonstrative.

After the longest stretch of silence so far, CorkyLee broke the quiet once again.

"Hey, Goud, when you're washing kitchen utensils and silverware, do you just wash the ends or do you also run the sponge up and down the handles?"

"I wash only the business end of any utensil. I never do the handle."

"Well, that settles it. I can't be with someone who doesn't wash the handles. You can just stop and let me out of the car right here."

"Really? You want me to stop?"

"Oh, Goudie, you silly duck. Can't you tell yet when I'm teasing you?" She relaxed back in the seat with a contented smile, looked straight ahead, and imagined olive-pit asphalt disappearing relentlessly under the truck.

*   *   *

Later that evening, we stopped for our fifth Lenny and Larry's cookie-and-coffee. After we got back on the road, CorkyLee said, "I *love* the songs that they play on Grossly Overplayed Classic Hits from the 1970s. Do you?"

I had nearly purposely driven over the guardrail and tumbled into a canyon below in order to avoid hearing "Hotel California" again, but through gritted teeth, I said, "Well, Cork, I sure do know Every. Single. Word. Of. Every. Song."

Trying to unclench my teeth in vain, I waited to see what the next song would be. I was pleased to hear the Elton John song, "Someone Saved My Life Tonight." My jaw relaxed a little as I pondered the line, "I would have walked head on into the deep end of the river."

I asked, "Hey, Cork, tell me. Do rivers have a deep end?"

"Gosh, let me think. Well, not really. Lakes have a deep *section*, but it's in the middle, not at the end, so you can't technically walk into the deep end of a lake unless there is a pier that extends out to the middle of it. But no, rivers don't have deep *ends*. One can't actually walk head-on into the deep *end* of a river."

"That's what I thought."

She asked, "You're confused about that Elton John lyric, aren't you? I have been, too! All these years I've been struggling to make sense of it. I suppose that when Elton was creating a melody to Bernie Taupin's lyrics, 'deep end of a pool' didn't fit, or it was too gruesome to sing, 'I would have walked head-on into the deep end of the pool.' So, I imagine that Elton called up Bernie and said, 'Hey, Bern. Can you change *pool* to something different? A word with two syllables would be splendid.' And Bernie said, 'Okay, Elt. How about *riv-er*?' Elton said, 'That's, great Bern, but rivers don't have deep ends.' Bernie said, 'Aww, Elt. No one will care. The fans love everything you do! The kids will buy boatloads of the record!'"

There was a long pause.

"Hey, there, Mr. Goudie Hawn, do you believe in a higher power?"

I snapped alert from envisioning myself as Elton John's bass player. "Yes, I do."

"I bet your higher power is a motorcycle racer or weightlifter or some sort of champion appliance repair person."

"No, I'm deeper than that. My higher power is the lowly but lovely snail. I think all snails are precious, but there's one mighty snail, the Grand Poohbah of snails, that oversees all creatures and sends snail love to everyone every day."

"Sounds far-fetched to me, GoudieDude. What about

the fact that people who grow vegetables and flowers *hate* snails because they eat the plants? Plus, there's a company that makes poison to kill snails called Corry's Slug & Snail Killer."

I cried out, "Oh, my goodness, no! Really? It seems that Corry isn't very evolved. I'm making a mental note to contact Corry and have a talk with him."

"Goud-o-rama, I have a question for you. Why do I cough when I stick a Q-tip in my ear?"

I didn't respond to CorkyLee's query because my map app suddenly told me to take the next exit. Could it be? Yes! I was happy and relieved to see that we were just minutes away from the grounds of the seminar venue. After spending more than six hours in a car with CorkyLee, I was now sure that I did not want to pursue a relationship with her. What a fruitcake! Mind you, she was a kind, good-hearted fruitcake, just not for me.

After finding a place to park my truck, we unrolled our sleeping bags by the light of the flashlight app on our phones. We slithered in for some quality outdoorsy sack time. Antithetical to our entire trip, CorkyLee didn't say a word as I snuggled into sleep. My eyelids felt as if they weighed two tons each. Just as they came crashing down, CorkyLee loudly whispered, "Hey, Goudie-Lee. I just made this up. Tell me if it's funny. I like to have toast with cream cheese and caveat for Sunday brunch."

I rolled my eyes and whispered, "Good night, CorkyLee, you goofy goose."

* * *

We awoke at seven the next morning, rolled up our bedding, and stashed it in the cab of the truck. I looked around and saw that we were situated on a lovely parcel of large-frond-fern-embellished forested land.

The event was advertised as a retreat. I said, "I'm assuming there will be groovy locally sourced, organic, vegetarian food served."

CorkyLee responded, "I imagine that there will be attractive, fit helpers meandering to and fro, wearing flowy, semi-see-through pastel clothing and bare midriffs."

We found a seat at the seminar and settled in. The speaker, named Farfugium, was indeed dynamic, attractive, and zestful. She announced that she preferred to be addressed as Doctor Farfugium but wouldn't mind if we called her Farfugee. She looked like a morning television show host and model: scary-good-looking and stunning in shape and proportion. In her giant mouth, her teeth appeared to be fluorescent and twice as big as a normal human's teeth.

As the morning went on, my arms got tired from hanging on her every word. All I could think about was the type and color of floor coverings she and I would have in our home, which we would occupy together when she wasn't on a speaking tour. While she was gone on these three- to four-week junkets, I would oversee the year-long remodel of our master bathroom, keep the yard trimmed, our pets fed, water her Angel Hair and Baby's Breath, and take out the trash each Monday morning. I would also maintain a high level of zeal for her during these long absences by not allowing stray thoughts of physical interaction with other humans to enter my mind. To accomplish this, four times a day I would look at pictures of four-wheel-drive truck accessories, carbon fiber tennis rackets, kite-surfing equipment, and garden drip watering system components.

When there was a fifteen-minute break in the seminar, I approached Dr. Farfugium and attempted to gain access to her good graces by saying, "Excuse me, Dr. Farfu-gee. We traveled a long way to get here. Does that make us far-from-home-ee?"

She giggled politely and glanced at my name tag. "Well, Goud, you know what they say about men who create puns?" I was delighted that she took an interest in me.

"No, Dr. Farfugee, what *do* they say?"

"I don't know, Goud. That's why I was asking *you*."

I burst out an awkward, fake-sounding guffaw. Dang it, I hoped I didn't offend her.

※ ※ ※

After the first day of classes, we ingurgitated our prepaid dinner of toasted, cinnamon-infused acorn hulls and Scarlet Queen turnip root tips.

"That was yummy!" declared CorkyLee. I detected a hint of irony and insincerity in her tone. I wasn't sure if the comment was supposed to be funny or if it required a response. I was hoping to withdraw from constantly interacting with CorkyLee so that others at the seminar would not see us as a couple.

As the dining hall emptied out, CorkyLee and I got up from the table and wandered out toward the parking lot. I intentionally slowed down so that she would get the hint to walk faster than my meandering pace and get ahead of me. I hoped to bump into an attendee who found me attractive and wanted to explore the inside of the gardener's shed together. But as I traipsed slowly toward my truck, CorkyLee also slowed down. No matter, because no one paid any attention to me by the time we reached the truck.

I opened the tailgate, and we unrolled our respective sleeping bags. As we got in and prepared for slumber, CorkyLee whispered expressionlessly, "Sleep tight and don't let the *Cimex lectulariuses* bite." I didn't respond. I thought it was clever, but I didn't want to lead her on. We lay there for a few minutes in blissful silence, then she whispered, "Goud. Hey, Goud."

I wasn't tired yet, so I said in a normal tone, "I'm still up."

"Oh, good. I was wondering. What's your opinion of rolled oats versus steel-cut oats?"

I had to softly chuckle at the randomness of her statement and the fact that, at least for this weekend, the universe had paired me with this quirky, odd, maddening, and maybe delightful fruitcake. I replied, "I don't have an opinion."

She said, "The reason I ask is that I read an article online that told me it's good for the skin to soak in a bathtub of hot water and oats. Rolled oats and steel-cut oats have distinctly different health advantages."

"Huh. How long do you soak?"

"A minimum of four days."

"I still don't have an opinion. Good night, CorkyLee," I said. I rolled over and closed my eyes.

"Good night, Goud-Boy."

In the morning we fumbled out of our sleeping bags, tumbled to the breakfast tent, mumbled about the coming day two talk, and stumbled over to the seminar yurt.

Dr. Farfugium looked even more yummy than the day before—oops, sorry. One of the self-help books that I actually *did* read—*Stop Crying in Your Sour Milk, You Big Baby*, written by Dr. Dayne Wyer and published by Specific House—advised readers to discontinue their habit of noticing people's physical attributes and see only their inner beauty, that no matter what their outward physical appearance, I was to focus on qualities such as spirituality, morality, integrity, honesty, loyalty, strength of character, generosity, and concern for one's fellow human. I loved being in Dr. Farfugium's presence and feeling her wonderful, guiding, benevolent energy and picturing the two of us kissing each other as we rolled around on a cushion of alfalfa strewn about the floor of a barn.

"Today we have a surprise guest!" Dr. Farfugium announced. "Actually, *two* surprise guests." The assembled audience perked up with anticipation. "Here with us today are two graduates of my program. They are shining examples of what you can achieve if you put my principles to work."

CorkyLee leaned over and whispered in my ear, "What program is she talking about?"

I whispered back, "I think this is where the speaker tells us that we can go only so far with what she is teaching this weekend. To actually turn our lives around, we will have to sign up for an expensive, ongoing program that includes months or even years of continuing training and its associated high costs."

"Oh, crap!" exclaimed CorkyLee.

"And now, allow me to introduce my special guests. Come out, come out, wherever you are!"

Two men with big, curly hairdos bounded out from behind a curtain. They both were smiling ear to ear as they each hugged Dr. Farfugium. Bursting with an almost manic energy, the two men introduced themselves.

"Hi, I'm Lenny!"

"What's up, everyone? I'm Larry!"

Then in unison, "We're Lenny and Larry of Lenny and Larry's cookie fame!"

Out of the corner of my eye I saw something move, then—oh, no! CorkyLee had crumpled into a heap on the floor. I got down on my knees to see what the matter was. "CorkyLee! Are you okay? Are you okay, Cork?"

Everyone around us had moved their chairs out of the way to give us room. My immediate impulse was to go into the mode of protector and partner. I rolled her onto her back and straightened out her arms so that her torso and hips were flat on the floor. I picked up her left hand and squeezed it while I straightened both her legs so that she would be as comfortable as possible.

Lenny and Larry were now standing over us, watching. CorkyLee's eyes opened. She looked around, then found my gaze and smiled. The group standing around us noticed this and began clapping and vocalizing their approval. CorkyLee looked up at Lenny and Larry and said, "If I had known you were coming, I would have baked a cookie." Everyone burst out laughing.

I looked around and said, "My precious CorkyLee seems to have fainted at the sight of her two heroes, Lenny and Larry." Lenny looked at me and said, "This is beautiful. The way you sprang into action could only have been out of love for your partner."

Larry said, "Lenny and I have made a lot of money using Dr. Farfugium's life and business advice, but what I really wish for is to have the kind of love you two have. I'd give away my cookie fortune in exchange for that."

I looked down at CorkyLee. She looked up at me and asked, "Did you just call me *precious*?"

I spoke to the crowd as I stared into her eyes. "She really isn't maddening, frustrating, annoying, or vexatious."

CorkyLee added, "Or any other names for Snow White's dwarves."

I shook my head and smiled. "Oh, CorkyLee, you goofy goose."

Lenny announced enthusiastically, "Hey! Who wants a Lenny and Larry's cookie?"

Larry added, "We brought a case of our wares and want to share. Does anyone care?"

There were shouts of "Yes! I want one!" and "Over here, please!" In a flash, all of the cookies were handed out to everyone except me. I wasn't concerned with cookies at the moment. I was pondering the possibilities of a new life with the precious CorkyLee.

As I adored her there, still lying on the floor, Lenny said, "Sorry that we didn't bring enough for you, Goud."

I looked up at him and said, "That's all right. I don't need cookies when I have CorkyLee."

CorkyLee raised herself up to a sitting position and looked into my eyes. "Oh, Goudie, you silly duck."

INDIETOP CHART

The net is riddled with music promotion scams that take advantage of gullible songwriters. I learned all about this topic more than ten years ago, and I still get come-on emails from bogus promo companies.

I had some fun with one recently. I submitted a "song" called "Hypertrophy Ain't Fur Sissies No More" by the artist Leisure Suit Paranoia. I didn't upload any song file, there was no song, I just entered a crazy song title and fake artist name that I made up on the spot. Here is the scam company's actual response, unedited:

> Hi Leisure Suit Paranoia,
> I am Christophe. I am the CEO of _____ Network based in Paris, France.
> You have a few hours ago submitted your song "Hypertrophy Ain't Fur Sissies No More." We have reviewed it. After listening to "Hypertrophy Ain't Fur Sissies No More," we have analyzed the chart potential with our tools. I contact you because your song "Hypertrophy Ain't Fur Sissies No More" has been nominated to

the Official Worldwide Independent Music Chart, "IndieTop Chart."

As an Official Chart, we monitor independent music all over the world in real time and your song "Hypertrophy Ain't Fur Sissies No More" by Leisure Suit Paranoia is currently highly playing on FM / DAB+TV, Satellite, Apple TV, Roku, Amazon Fire TV, Samsung TV, and Android TV and many other streaming platforms like Spotify and YouTube.

You seem to benefit from a very awesome music promotion and we congratulate you! Congrats!

Your song "Hypertrophy Ain't Fur Sissies No More" is now ready to become charted in the Worldwide Official Chart of The Independent Music: "IndieTop Chart." Exposure all over the world!

As a nominated Independent Artist today, you will be able to participate in this official chart and may receive the physical plaque trophy awarded to the best monthly performance. Incredible!

"IndieTop Chart" is also a radio show broadcast every week on more than 800 stations around the world and also a TV show broadcast by Satellite and on the major streaming media platforms (Apple TV, Roku, Amazon Fire TV, Android TV, Samsung TV).

To validate your nomination now, simply follow the setup process by clicking here:

Let's go! You are now on the road to success!

Warm Regards,

Christophe.

Note to the reader: If you're a music creator and put music out on the mighty interweb, watch out. If you haven't been scammed yet, you likely will be at some point. We artists typically learn our lessons by doing it wrong the first time. But don't be afraid to try. Remember: You can't be a wiener if you don't play the game! :-)

PULL THE LEVER . . . NOW!

I have a sweet, personable friend named Glendina. After years working as a customer service specialist for a landscape materials company, Glendina was fired through no fault of her own. (Well, read on, dear reader, and you decide.) One day a moronic customer called to complain that the shipment of pea gravel to his front yard was wrong.

"Waddaya mean, it's *wrong*?" she inquired.

The customer hollered into the phone, "I ordered pea gravel, but this gravel is too damn big! I wanted small pebbles! Ya know?! Like a pea! That's why I ordered *pea* gravel! Pea! Pea! PEA!"

Glendina lost it and said, "I'm so sorry, sir. We made a mistake and sent you a load of *urine* gravel, not *pea* gravel, so why doncha go piss off!"

Glendina had imagined for years that someday she would work in the exciting airline industry. After she left the landscape materials company, she answered an ad on GlamorousAirportJobsForUdotcom. Finally, at age thirty-two, she was applying for the job of her dreams. She passed the interview at the airport and was hired.

On her first day, Glendina was led to the underside of a passenger plane. A cargo door was open, and luggage was being loaded. Her superior, Wandita, led her through this cargo door to a smaller compartment, the size of a typical small residential bathroom. "Come on in, Glendina," smiled Wandita. Glendina cautiously stepped inside, surveying the room. There was a cozy-looking padded chair. Next to the chair were the handles of two long levers, approximately four feet long, that were attached to two enormous metal tanks. Situated in the floor between the chair and the levers was a three-foot-square glass window.

"Your job is to sit in this chair, wear these headphones, and listen for commands," said Wandita.

Excited and curious, Glendina said, "Okay! What kinds of commands will I be listening for?"

Wandita cooly answered, "The control center will tell you when to pull the levers. The red lever releases simple, harmless moisture, which condenses in the cold air and produces vapor that hangs in the atmosphere. The blue lever releases poisonous gases that we use to control the masses."

"Oh, gosh!" blurted Glendina. "I'm aware of this contentious debate, of course. It's been the crux of violent altercations between chem-trail deniers and believers."

"That's right," Wandita replied matter-of-factly. "Now you and the president know the truth. You will, of course, be required to sign an NDA."

"My brother contracted NDA when he was little and had to wear leg braces."

Wandita pursed her lips and shook her head. "No, a nondisclosure agreement, you ninny! If you ever tell anyone about what really goes on inside the bellies of airplanes, we will seek out your loved ones, tie them up with fresh, organic buckwheat spaghetti noodles, and tickle their private parts with a feather from a yellow-bellied tit sniffer!"

"All right, then," Glendina agreed. "I certainly will never tell a soul. I don't want my relatives to undergo that kind of horrendous punishment. But maybe someday after work you and I could..."

"No!" Wandita shouted. "No employee fraternizing, even after work!" She then winked, smiled, and handed Glendina a card with her phone number. "I promise to be gentle," she whispered. Glendina raised her eyebrows, smiled, and placed the card in her pocket.

She asked, "Why is there a window in the floor?" Wandita snapped back to supervisor mode. "You will be required to learn the lay of the land that is below all your flights. You have to constantly look down and follow the topography. When you are given a command to pull the poison lever, you have to know if you have relatives living in that area. If you do, pull the harmless red moisture lever."

"Or if I don't like a certain relative, I might pull the poison blue lever," Glendina chuckled.

Wandita shook her head. "No, no. Let's not be silly." Then she smiled and whispered, "Let's save that for later."

Glendina winked, then said in a mock-serious tone, "Okay, then, let me recap. I listen for commands in my headphones. I look down through the window in the floor and follow the terrain below. If I get a command to pull the poison lever, I check to see if I know anyone down there. If I don't, I let 'er rip! If I know anyone there, I pull the harmless moisture lever. Is that correct?"

"You got it, babe!" Wandita exclaimed. "I mean, you got it, new recruit Glendina."

Glendina asked, "Just out of curiosity, how many people work in this department?"

"Actually, just the two of us. I am your supervisor, technically, but we work as a team. You and I will be on every flight together."

"Oh, good! I think we will become buddies and be a great team!"

Wandita responded, "I hope so, as we will travel many miles and spend many, many hours together."

Glendina winked at her new supervisor again and said, "By the way, Wandita, in my spare time, I write jokes. I just fabricated one in my head, and it was inspired by you."

Wandita brightened. "Well, I must hear it then!"

"Okay, Supervisor Wandita. A woman whose job was to manage people had a very large sun shield custom-made that attached to a hat. It was shiny and fantastically colorful. When she put it on her head, she could flip a switch on it and fly! Do you know what it was, Wandita?"

Wandita shook her. "I have no clue. Why don't you go ahead and tell me."

Glendina was so excited that she started noticeably vibrating. She was smiling so hard that her cheeks hurt. She struggled to keep from exploding in gleeful, howling laughter. Then, with as much of a poker face as she could muster, Glendina said, "It was a supervisor."

Wandita stood motionless and expressionless. Glendina said, "Do you get it? *Super*-visor!" Without missing a beat, Wandita turned, pointed to the exit door, and said, "Get out of the airplane, walk across the tarmac back to the terminal, walk out through the parking lot, find your car, get in, and leave. Don't ever come back here again."

Glendina never did sign that NDA, and now you know the truth.

THE BUSHY BROWN BEARDS

Several years ago, I was desperate to make money in an unconventional way. I believe I was predestined to skirt normality and live not a pragmatic but a prismatic life.

I got the brilliant idea to create an income stream by starting an internet business with the completely irrelevant, non sequitur title, Overcooked Broccoli. My business had nothing to do with food, but I figured it was a catchy name for a web-based business that got crappy, wannabe music bands semi-legitimate spins on various internet streaming platforms.

To make a profit, I hired a lovely person through Fiverr named Wazlcpeoh, who was in Botswana. (Fiverr is a global online marketplace for freelance services.) Wazlcpeoh promised me that each song would receive 5,000 streams for five dollars, 10,000 streams for ten dollars, and so on. I charged each band fifty dollars to generate 5,000 streams, seventy-five dollars for 7,500 streams, and so on. I made thousands of dollars each month from all the eager-for-quick-fame, gullible musicians who fell for my clever internet ads, which promised them stardom and opulence from all the streaming royalties they would receive. Simultaneously, because I'm old and frustrated that I myself didn't make it big as a music star when I was young, I formed a college-aged music band that played songs I had written. They were tunes I had written for me to sing, but I had become geriatric and frightful to look at. Who would want to see or hear me?

My fabricated group comprised two women and two men, all of whom were younger than twenty-two. Under my tutelage, the two men were required to let their facial hair sprout, while the two women wore false lumberjack beards for their public appearances. (Their contract with me stated that the women were never to be seen in public without the false facial hair and that the men were forbidden to shave.) I called the band the Bushy Brown Beards. Technically, they were employees of Overcooked Broccoli, LLC. Any income that was generated flowed first into the company bank account, then to the four puppets—I mean people—via weekly paychecks.

I recorded, engineered, and produced their first album, *My Beard Is Running for President*, at Sylvia Massy's incredible Oregon-based studio. I wish I would have let her produce it. I'm such a control freak and egomaniac that I declined to pay her very affordable producer fee because I thought I could do better myself. Now I know that I ruined it. All the songs fell flat and lacked the amazing, magical, multi-dimensional sparkle and shine that Sylvia is known for.

One day during rehearsal in Sylvia's studio, I lost my cool in front of the band and accused them of not performing well enough. I shouted profanities and hollered, "I don't hear any gall-dang hits!" Privately, I admitted to myself that it was not their fault. After all, they were playing *my* songs the way *I* had written and arranged them. But my ego was such that I had to blame *them*. I screamed, flew into a rage, and punched a wall.

During the madness and fury of my tantrum, with gallons of adrenaline surging through my body, I couldn't feel pain in the shattered phalanges of my hand. I continued to berate them while I scanned the room for something to hurl or smash. My eyes fell upon Sylvia's prized antique German-British Blattnerphone tape machine. My neck veins bulging, I struggled and strained to pick up the device, then lurched over to the nearest open window. With Herculean might, I shoved it out the fenestration, and it plummeted into the pool, six stories below. Next, I grabbed a prized 1957 Mudguard bass guitar, flung it mercilessly to the floor, and jumped up and down on it. I stopped only because I noticed there were no band members in the room to witness this spectacular act. They had quietly slinked out when I was watching the tape machine *ka-ploosh* into the swimming pool.

* * *

I figured that even with a dud of a recording, I could get the songs played. I was spending all the money that I made from the wannabe bands to promote the Bushy

Brown Beards. I had our buddy, Wazlcpeoh, on retainer, and agreed to pay twice the normal fee if she/he/it would hype the songs with extra zeal. I had no idea who Wazlcpeoh was or even if there was an actual human behind the interesting name. Whatever she/he/it was, she/he/it fiercely pushed the ditties on Spotify, Deezer, Apple Music, and Amazon Music, and even got the music spins on good old-fashioned radio. Sadly, after spending an anesthesiologist's one-year salary on promoting it, no one gave a rat's rectum about the music.

I spent many tens of thousands of dollars on setting up live gigs at all the hot-spot entertainment venues in populated cities. For example, I called the booking agent at the 40-Watt Club in Athens, Georgia, and told her that the Bushy Brown Beards were going on tour and would be in her area in April, and that we needed a Saturday night gig. After getting past the usual, "Who are you? What's the name of the band again? We only book well-known bands on Friday and Saturday nights. I can give you a Monday night at one a.m.," I asked her what it would cost to rent the entire venue with staff. "Oh. Well, let's see. Hall rental from five p.m. to three a.m., lighting person, sound person, ticket takers, setup and cleaning crew, security. Oh, and electricity usage. Special price for you today of twenty-five thousand dollars." I cheerfully chirped, "Done!"

I proceeded to rent venues in all the major cities and organized local street teams of college and high school kids to ensure that the venues were filled to capacity. How did I do this, you ask? I gave my team members tickets to hand out that were not only for free admission but were guaranteed to pay each person twenty-five dollars if they stayed for the entire show. The tickets promised an additional ten dollars if the crowd rallied and demanded an encore. I also paid local press and radio people to attend and offered a bonus if they wrote and announced positively about the Bushy Brown Beards' performance. But after all that expense, like consuming a case of Miller Lite beer, my promotion didn't create a lasting buzz.

I had borrowed and spent $600,000 to finance the project, and my loan was coming due. You may wonder how in the holy-moly mother-of-pearl I found someone to advance me six hunny G's. Read on and I'll 'splain it to you.

* * *

The Bushy Brown Beards were playing at a little club one night when in walks Razz Peacock, the flamboyant and ostentatious drummer in one of the most popular rock groups in the world, Abstain from Abstinence. No kidding! Razz *freaking* Peacock!

He tentatively strolled the club, looking for a place to sit. His appearance and apparel differed from his usual crazy clothes, wild hair, and garish jewelry that he always wore when he appeared on stage or in pictures. Razz carried himself like an ordinary, average club-goer. He wasn't the condescending, attention-seeking, make-way-for-the-king snobbish self that rock fans knew. Mr. Peacock radiated noticeably vulnerable approachability.

I took this observation as a sign that I should engage him in conversation while I had the chance.

I furtively sidled over and tried to catch his attention. Razz seemed to be enjoying the Bushy Brown Beards' performance, so I leaned over and casually informed him that I was their manager. He smiled and piped up, "Hey, man, this band is mondo abundant!" I thought I was up on all the latest slang and lingo (*slingo*?) but hadn't yet heard *abundant* used in that way.

"Thank you. In fact, they're playing *my* songs. Songs that I wrote for them."

"Really?" Razz said. "I'm impressed! They're cool tunes. I like the hooks and bridges." I couldn't believe what I heard! Finally, I received acknowledgment from an industry professional (and a big star, mind you!) for my hard work. I had spent hours crafting each of the songs, creating catchy instrumental parts and clever irresistible bridges. In fact, If I may allow myself to boast, I felt my bridges were as good as any of the great bridges created by Barry Gibb, Ralph Modjeski, Carole King, Thomas Telford, Sting, and Santiago Calatrava.

Propped up by Razz's kind and sincere words, I couldn't help but reveal the dispiriting truth that the songs weren't actually doing that well out in the real world. "I have to tell you, Mr. Peacock, as hard as it is to believe, the Bushy Brown Beards just haven't caught on with the public. Our spins have plateaued on the streaming platforms and radio, man."

Razz replied with concern, "I don't understand. These songs are little gems, and the band is great!"

I agreed and confessed, "I think I've Peter Principled out."

Razz said, "Oh, I know that term. You've risen to the top of your level of incompetence, right?"

"Yes!" I cried. "I've tried and tried, and now I cry uncle. I believe that with better promotion, a publicist, a marketing company, and a booking agent who can get them into some high-profile gigs, they would take off! I'm certain the payback is there, but I just don't have the brains or financial brawn that they need."

Mr. Peacock turned and looked me squarely in the eyes. "Well, great balls of cookie dough! I have some cashola to invest! I agree with your prediction that the Bushy Brown Beards are going to blow up. Do you mind if I call them the BBBs?"

I gagged, inhaling some saliva. After a mild coughing fit, I said, "No, sir, I don't mind at all. You can call them anything you want, just don't call them late for lunch." I kept a poker face to see if he got my stupid pun.

"I'll give you my phone number," he said. "Text me to set up a meeting, and we'll throw down some numbers."

I beamed. "You got it, Mr. Peacock!"

He got up to leave. "Oh, keep your day job. Leave the jokes to the professionals."

✼ ✼ ✼

I was cat-curious as to how Razz had become a down-to-earth, congenial person. He was so congenial that I thought maybe he was congenitally congenial. (In fact, if you were to rub his congenitals in a specific way, his congeniality would swell and oscillate. But during this state, he would not be fertile because he had been ostracized after his fifth child was born.)

I wanted to know more about Razz and his seemingly sudden switch from standoffish to sociable. I called my friend Curtis Smith, who keeps his toes on the pulse of the music industry. He's the Grand Poohbah of Maelstrom Music Publicity.

"Curtis, my main man! How goes the melee?"

"Is this the Goud of thunder, Goud of light, rocking and rolling most every night?!"

"Yes, my fine feathered friend! And like a curious lumberjack, I need to axe you a question."

Curtis was his typical cheerful self. "Sure thing. Putz your wuzzle? I mean, what's your puzzle?"

"Believe it or not, I recently bumped into the one and only Razz Peacock in the audience at a Bushy Brown Beards show."

"Okay, okay. I gotcha. I was his press agent in the '80s when Rick Rubin produced the two best Abstain from Abstinence albums."

I was impressed. "Wow, Curtis! Cool. Was Sylvia Massy the engineer on those sessions?"

"Yep. She sure was. Rick is a genius, of course, but I feel Razz's drum sound and the reason fans still adore the band is largely due to Sylvia's work on those records."

"I hear you, Curtis! I can certainly dig in the garden that you've planted."

"Um, Goud?"

"Yeah, Curtis?"

"You're a freakin' dork."

"Aww, Curtis. Thanks! Oh, hey, the reason I called is that I talked to Razz at the show, and he was nice and even, dare I say, friendly. We talked for a while, and he wants to help me promote the Bushy Brown Beards. Can I trust him? Has he really changed?"

He replied, "I thought everyone had heard."

"Heard what?"

"That he found a god or goddess or a guru or someone like that. He bought an island and opened a detox center for people addicted to being seen in busy coffee shops. The god-guru guy convinced him to give away his cars and houses. Razz lives in the smallest guest room with only a bed, a nightstand, and a candle for reading autobiographies of famous high school home economics teachers. He has rejected the carnal pursuit of intimate relations with women. Ironically, he now has fourteen platonic female roommates who share the home with him."

I was speechless for a moment, then, "Curtis, are you kidding?! Everything you just said really happened?"

"Yep. It really did!"

"Well, I guess he kept some of his money because he told me to call him and hammer out a deal where he's gonna float me a loan."

*　*　*

Let's fast-forward the story a bit. I met with the inimbulable, um, untimateable, I mean, inanimantle... oh, crap! I took a meeting with the *uncopyable* Razz Peacock, and he agreed to advance me six hundred thousand bucks! We both felt confident that that amount would surely get us some major airplay for the Bushy Brown Beards and bust them wide open into the consciousness of the world's populace. Razz left it up to me to administer the mound of money and oversee the various arms of the promotion and marketing effort.

The sad factuality is that I spent the entire lot of loot within a year but received scant positive exposure. The terms of payback contained the names of three of Snow White's many dwarves: Vague, Nebulous, and Hazy. In fact, I couldn't be certain that Razz wanted to be paid back at all. We didn't even handshake on it, we only high-fived.

One day, the adorable Matilda, lead singer of the Bushy Brown Beards, texted me. *How R we doing? Should we hang in w/you?* By now I knew the whole thing was doomed. Deflated, I called her. "Hey Tilda. The truth is, I paid for a Sunset Boulevard billboard, a Times Square jumbotron, internet and magazine ads, and I bribed radio DJs in nearly every state and province in North America to spin the tracks. I couldn't afford to buy prime radio time; that would have wiped out all the money in one week. I metered out the cash for a three-month airplay campaign at each station but had to settle for the two a.m. to six a.m. slot. You remember that tour you guys did opening for Abstain from Abstinence?"

"Yep, I sure do," she said.

"I paid seventy-five grand to get that gig for the Bushy Brown Beards. Razz said he couldn't get me the 'friend deal,' so I had to pay his management company full price."

"Oh, wow!" she exclaimed. "I didn't know you had to *pay* for that! It was a crappy experience. They threw full cans of Red Bull at us! We got booed offstage at every gig!" I was even more depressed now. I said, "I realize that. I was there, remember?" Matilda tossed her phone on her bed without ending call.

* * *

One late evening I got a text from Razz. *Yo Goud-ee-o! What up? Got any biscuits to slip my way?* I knew what he meant. It had been more than a year now, and he was being nice, dropping hints about being paid back. *Razzmatazz! How you be?* I texted back. *Biscuits be poppin' out da oven soon 4U!* That was a lie. I had no idea where any "biscuits" would come from, let alone six hundred thousand of them.

* * *

In the year since Mr. Peacock slid the money under my door for music promotion, he had fallen more deeply under his guru's spell.

Let me fill you in, my fine reader, on some details. The guru had set up a legal charity called I'm the Guru, So Don't Ask Why. He had convinced Razz to sign over his five houses, sixteen motorcycles, and all twenty-three of his cars to the charity. One of the houses, an eight-bed, six-bath mansion in the charming North River neighborhood in Toledo, Ohio, was set up as the guru's headquarters, office, and home. Razz occupied the small fourth-floor guest room. (The guru had persuaded Razz to pay the charity $7,500 a month in rent.) The fourteen young adult female followers flitted about the magnificent abode all hours of night and day while the music of Cole Porter wafted endlessly from the elaborate whole-house sound system.

For a time, Razz felt it was the perfect heavenly hideout, a place where he could rest and restore his energies while he studied the guru's lessons on nutrition, exercise, spirituality, and abstinence.

"Drinking a heaping tablespoon of your own urine each day is good for you," chirped a sprightly woman in the hallway one morning as Razz walked to the kitchen.

"Performing 350 consecutive squats three times a week increases my thigh-gap!" alerted another young disciple.

A tall, round-faced, round-bottomed woman cheerfully announced on the patio one afternoon, "In the last two years alone, I've attended ninety-three weekend seminars with such titles as Trash Collectors Are the Deliverers of Hope; Jealousy in Your Past Lives: Use It to Monitor Your Love Interests; and Learn to Destroy Your Mental Hangups from People Who Were Mean to You by Envisioning Tickling Their Genitals with Barbed Wire."

As the year wore on, the guru increasingly wormed his way into Razz's finances. During a particularly weak and vulnerable time for him, Razz fell to the sway of the guru's sweet talk for a month.

"Mr. Peacock, if you sign this document, you will have even fewer troubles than you did yesterday," the guru advised. It was a contract that transferred 100 percent ownership of Razz's music royalty stream to the guru's hastily set up music publishing company, Sneaky Bass-Tard Songs, LLC. Razz was still on his "simplify" kick and didn't dilly-dally in delivering his designation on the dotted delineation.

"I can't thank you enough, Guru," he uttered as he pushed the contract back across the table toward his life coach.

"Being free of this fiscal ball and chain will bring you happiness. You have made a wise choice."

The only money Razz had left was whatever savings he'd had in his bank account before his association with the guru. It was nothing at which to expel mucous-laden air through one's nostrils, as it was a rather nice passel of more than three million pieces of eight. But if we realistically analyze Mr. Peacock's daily dispersal of ducats, it occurs to me that maybe three million nori sheets wouldn't last too long. Consider that Razz had developed not only a fear of flying but also a fear of riding on buses. He wasn't touring anymore and had no source of income without his royalties. Unlike his much wiser band mates, he hadn't purchased any apartment buildings or shopping centers with his share of Abstain from Abstinence profits. He had followed the financial advice of his middle-class parents to a point. He had bought five houses (good), yet they were all very large, architecturally odd, and in exclusive areas (bad: high property taxes, insurance, and maintenance, and hard to rent or sell).

Any money over and above what he had paid for his five houses (that wasn't pissed away on cars, motorcycles, helicopter ski trips, and filling his basketball-arena-sized barn with every Ludwig drum set he could get his hands on) he deposited in a regular checking account. In other words, even before he met the guru he was rapidly losing his nest egg.

I met him at just the right time, when his letting go of six hundred thousand of those aforementioned pieces of coinage was not a threat to his guru-influenced reduced lifestyle. Cloaked in sweet deceit and with a disingenuous, perfidious, mendacious, and prevaricating-yet-exigent (and many other big words that no one actually uses in real life) manner, the guru continued with his crystal blue persuasion of Razz, attempting to subtly extricate every last drop of legal tender.

※ ※ ※

After that first timid text that I received from Razz, a series of four or five increasingly demanding (yet passive-aggressive) messages came in from him over a period of ten days. He repeated his request that I start paying back the loan. With each text, I sent back lame responses that were intended to stall for more time. Then one foggy New Year's Eve, he called. His voice had changed completely. Gone was any hint of warmth or cordiality. It was chilling. I felt as though I didn't know him at all and that he didn't have a clue who I was. It was literally like he had become the Razz-Peacock-Abstain-from-Abstinence-drummer-person I had read about and seen on TV. I hadn't known him then, so I was shocked when I heard his voice in my phone.

"Goud. Stop. Think. Where's my money? What the freakin' heck do you think you're doing? I'm not giving you a month to pay me back in full. I'm not giving you two weeks. I'm telling you that I WANT ALL THE DADDY-HUMPING MONEY RIGHT NOW!!" He screamed that last sentence so loud that it permanently damaged my phone speaker. I didn't know what to say. I was afraid of upsetting him, but I was hoping I could appeal to his sense of humor—if he still had one.

I calmly asked, "What's *daddy-humping money?*"

"Daddy-humping! Daddy-humping! Daddy-humping! You know? With a hyphen between *daddy* and *humping*."

I let him rant and didn't say anything.

"Are you that stupid? Daddy *hyphen* humping money!" I still didn't get it and remained silent.

He settled down a bit. "Okay. It's like *motherfucking* money but more politically correct."

"Oh. Okay. I get it now," I said calmly. There was an awkward four seconds of silence, then he spoke.

"Aw, Goud. Sorry to clamp a vice grip on your nuts, but I really need to be paid back. Like, soon. I mean, like, in a week. Dig me?"

I nodded my head, then realized he couldn't see me and said, "I dig you like a ditch."

✷ ✷ ✷

I later learned, from my all-knowing music biz pal Curtis Smith of Maelstrom Music Publicity, that Razz had partaken in an ayahuasca ceremony led by the guru. While under the influence of the South American psychoactive and entheogenic brewed drink, Mr. Peacock had dreamed of the purest, most blissful existence he could possibly attain.

It was the life he knew he was meant to live and his greatest contribution to society. After he woke up, turned his head, and projectile vomited all over the guru's shoes, Razz had announced, "I'm *supposed* to be living an extravagant life! I know that I was tagged at birth by our great creator to set an outrageous example for the common people of the world to keep them working, paying taxes, and foolishly hoping to someday have at least a pint-sized resemblance of my life."

Curtis said, "Razz kicked the guru and all the young women to the proverbial curb. He's in a legal battle now to regain ownership and possession of all his houses, cars, motorcycles, and royalties."

* * *

After the phone call from Razz demanding payment in full, the reality of my failed attempt at promoting the BBBs hoisted its pretty head. That evening, Matilda, physically the smallest of the four Bushy Brown Beards, texted me. *Need 2 meet asap. 2nite please?* I agreed to see them.

The four hairy twenty-somethings were present when I arrived in the basement studio that I had provided for them. Matilda spoke up. "We've become artistically frustrated. We want to write and play our own songs now."

I couldn't take the double-whammy stress of Razz's call and this news. I screamed at them, "Who is your freakin' papa?! Who made you all world-famous millionaires?!"

"But we're not famous *or* millionaires," Matilda calmly said. "We can't live on fifty dollars a week anymore. We want to leave you and start our own band."

I stormed out of the room, walked back to my apartment/office, and initiated legal action against them for breach of contract. I distributed a press release that I was suing them. The next day I texted Matilda, then walked over to the BBBs basement to inform them of the impending litigation. Only Matilda was there. "The others went out for a walk," she said. In reality, they were quivering in the bathroom, ears pressed to the door.

"I saw your post on Instagram," she said. "How are we supposed to gather up $65 million to pay you? Besides that, we are tuckered out from you controlling us. Three of us are sick of being kept in this dark basement apartment, subsisting on only the wheat milk, tofu, powdered quail kidney, and the lima bean protein shakes that you feed us."

I asked, "Who is the fourth member, the one who doesn't oppose your regimen?"

"Jerezikial," she replied. "Our bass player—of course, right? He's the oddball. He feels deserving of punishment for being born beautiful and talented. In fact, we only recently learned that he's been pretending to be broke so that he'll bond better with me and the other two Beards. He's living on monthly disbursements from a forkoverable trust."

"What? What kind of trust?"

"You've heard of a revocable trust? Well, his family set up a forkoverable trust. You know, like, 'fork over the money.'"

I chuckled. "You're funny, Tilda."

"No, really. It's an actual trust thing. Go ahead and Google it."

"I don't need to look it up. I believe you."

I quickly dropped my pleasant demeanor and got back to being the heavy. I sneered and told her through clenched teeth, "Okay, missy Matilda! You and the others better get ready for the challenge of your lives! I'll take this all the way to the super court!"

The corners of Matilda's mouth started to curl up. She tried but couldn't contain a smile.

I hollered at her, "What's so freakin' funny?!"

She let go a laugh. "You said *super court* instead of *supreme court*."

"I did *not* say that!"

"Yep. You said, 'I'll take this to the *super court*.'"

She was so adorably cute that I felt my anger melting away. I began to smile, "Are you sure?"

"Yes! You did! You said *super court*. Super court." She jumped up, punched the air with her fist, and shouted, "SUPER COURT!"

She was precious, charming, and delightful. I had often had visions of the two of us running away to Grand Canary Island, off the coast of Northwest Africa. We would live out our remaining years (her approximately sixty-three remaining and my approximately twenty-three remaining) as a sun- and water-worshipping couple, strolling the beaches hand in hand. Our home would be a dilapidated apartment above a bakery that opened at three thirty every morning, with loud, clanging, clunking sounds of workers opening and closing walk-in refrigerator doors, mixing dough, firing up ovens, and blasting dance music. The flour and other ingredients would attract rats, roaches, and large spiders that would be curious what was on the floor above and investigate our apartment frequently.

I eventually stopped my day fantasy when, like a Bowery bum who finally realizes the bottle is empty and there is nothing left, I grasped our age difference. She was twenty-two and I was sixty-two. Was forty years too much of a gap? At this age, I'm still functioning at a high level with regard to the things that matter most in a relationship. Like many men, I know what women want from us: to sit next to them while we watch TV, take them out to dinner once a week, achieve erections, and squirt reproductive fluid during physical pleasure sessions. Right?

When Matilda was in her prime of, say, thirty-eight, I would be seventy-eight. Not too bad. But then, when she was forty-eight and I was eighty-eight? Her at fifty-eight, me at ninety-eight? I would probably have erectile dysfunction by then and require a VCD penis pump. It's likely that our conversations would descend to my endless reminiscences about the Bee Gees, the Cincinnati Reds, Farrah Fawcett, the Dallas Cowboys cheerleaders, my cherished 1973 Yamaha 100 dirt bike, and my 1978 senior year of high school.

My anger was defused after seeing Matilda jump and shout SUPER COURT! I couldn't stay mad. "Okay," I said, "I'll drop my lawsuit. Will you help me pay back the $600,000 I borrowed? I really *did* think you four were the next big thing."

Matilda tilted her head to one side, blinked, smiled, turned around, and walked toward the kitchen. Was that a yes or a no? As if being told to turn around after a count of three by a movie director, she turned around after, well, a count of three. "We'll do what we can to help you." I felt a rush of hope. "We'll stick with you, but you must stop force-feeding us those horrid protein shakes and let us live on pizza, ice cream, cheap white wine, and cigarettes, like a normal band."

"Okay," I replied.

I called the press editor of *Tumbling Pebble*, the most influential music magazine in the world, to let her know that I had dropped my lawsuit against the Bushy Brown Beards. She said, "Who are you? We've never heard of that group."

Crap! I forgot that the band hadn't caught on with the public. I abruptly ended the call.

The band had no value and no way for me to make money off them to pay back my loan. My Overcooked Broccoli, LLC business scam couldn't possibly bring in six hundred thousand bucks. I got the idea to release outtakes of the band's recording sessions. It included the band members making embarrassing mistakes on their instruments, burping, goofing around, and banging away, making painfully cacophonic fragments of music in a songwriting session. This would be something that people would consume by the shipload if they had been the Beatles. But not one gander was taken at my internet ads for Bloopers, Boners, and Blunders by the Bushy Brown Beards. Not a single soul clicked the link.

* * *

Then I remembered I knew the masseur for the shoeshine woman for the chauffeur for a famous food industry person, who might see value in the Bushy Brown Beards and pass me some greenbacks to pay off my Mr. Peacock obligation. I looked in my phone contacts, and yes! I found Mattias the masseur.

I called Mattias and presented my situation. "I hear you, Goud, old pal. Tough times these are, indeed. Let me call my gal, Shiloh the shoe shiner. I'll see if she'll talk to you." In an hour, the ringtone on my phone (Debbie Boone singing "You Light Up My Life") sounded, indicating a call was coming through. It was Mattias the masseur. He said, "Shiloh the shoe shiner sounded happy to help, told me to give you her number and give her a call."

I tapped the number into my keypad and pressed the green Call button. It rang only once, and Shiloh the shoe shiner answered. She was kindly and empathetic. "Oh, gosh, Goud. I feel your pain. I was in a band in the '80s. We never quite made it, either. I hope you and the Bushy Brown Beards work things out and go big! Here's Charvik the chauffeur's number. Give him a call."

I was a little nervous to cold-call Charvik the chauffeur, so I texted him. He responded ten minutes later. *A frnd Shiloh is frnd mine. Call please.* I called him immediately and presented my predicament. Charvik the chauffeur's broken English was charming.

"I hear saying need money pay loan, correct?"

I wasn't sure if he could comprehend my *actual* plight or if he just wanted to help me because I was referred by Shiloh the shoe shiner. I slowly said, "Yes. Need pay loan soon. I mean, I need to pay back my loan soon."

"Okay. I talk my boss. I call today-night."

I asked, "Do you mean you'll call your *boss* today-night or call *me* today-night?"

"I call me today-night."

I assumed he meant I call *you* today-night. I walked to a nearby city park's shallow reflecting pool, took off my shoes, rolled up my pant legs, and waded anxiously for him to call back.

In the meanwhile, I called Mattias the masseur to ask for more details on the famous food industry person who was only three degrees of separation away.

"She started her career as a potato peeler at the Wild Goose Café and Bar in Ashland, Oregon," Mattias said. "She was so good at that task, she never got promoted. The owner was very supportive and checked in with her frequently, but she repeatedly declined to climb the folding step stool of success."

"Fascinating," I said. "Go on."

Mattias the masseur continued, "Her name was an aptronym. [An *aptronym* is a name that aptly suits its owner.] Flay Tuber. So of course she ended up a potato peeler!"

"Crazy!" I said. "Did her parents do that on purpose?"

"I don't know. She out-peeled not only every other restaurant worker but also those fancy potato-peeling machines. At the NRWO [National Restaurant Workers Olympics], Flay was the potato-peeling champion eight years in a row! After winning her eighth and final Golden Spud Scraper trophy, she quit the Wild Goose to accept an offer to be the figurehead of a chain of potato-based restaurants called The Lusty Russet. Flay Tuber earned a salary for appearing in all their advertising and made public appearances across the country."

"Did she also take a percentage of the profits?" I asked.

"Yes! Flay was cagey, canny, and crafty. She negotiated a 15 percent stake."

I couldn't avoid the setup and deadpanned, "A 15 percent stake in a potato restaurant?" Mattias the masseur didn't flinch. I guess he didn't like pun humor.

"Thank you for the backstory on Flay Tuber. Mattias the masseur, you da best!"

He quickly interjected, "But wait, there's more! Flay has an insatiable lust for life and love. Be careful that she doesn't fall in love with you—unless you want that."

Curious now, I said, "Okay, tell me more."

"In 1989, Ms. Tuber became involved with actor Shine Boligrafo following his divorce from the dazzling flippant, fugaciously sycophantic, and deliciously lubricious toll booth attendant, Fee Taker. Flay was by then a celebrity in her own right and was offered multiple acting roles by various movie studios. She accepted the job of portraying

Maid Marion Michael Morrison in the cooking-themed film *Robin Colander: Prince of Sieves* but then had to turn it down because she became pregnant with her and Mr. Boligrafo's child.

"After a sudden, cyclonic relationship following a colonic irrigation in July 2003, Ms. Tuber married the celebrity irrigation-technician-to-the stars Getty Allout in September 2003. Sadly, their union did not pan out, and within three months they had purged all remnants of matrimony from their convivial cave."

"Wow!" I exclaimed. "I will keep all that in mind when dealing with her. Thank you!"

Mattias the masseur said, "You are very welcome, and I hope to see you somewhere down the road on the gameboard of life."

* * *

I stepped out of the reflecting pool to sit on a bench and let my feet dry, then walked back to my comfortably crummy and crumbly third-floor hobble-up hovel where Lexington crosses 47th Street.

At around nine o'clock that evening, Debbie Boone's voice started to sing from my phone. I swiped right while she was mid-chorus, "Yooooo liiiight uuup—"

"Hi, this is Goud."

"Hello I talk now."

I grinned 1609.34 meters wide. "Charvik the chauffeur! So glad you called!"

"My boss Flay Tuber say call ten today-night."

"Oh! In one hour, right?"

"Yes. Text first, two-one-three-three-five-five-eight-four-five-three."

I was giddy with hope. "Thanks a million, Charvik the chauffeur! I owe you!"

"Is okay no problem I talk later."

At three minutes past ten, I texted the great Flay Tuber. That seemed the right amount of time to not appear too eager, whereas waiting four or five minutes seemed flippantly too long. She probably wasn't actually waiting for me to text, right? Ms. Tuber's brain was presumably completely full with high-level, crucial, critical, decision-making matters. I would bet that she had already forgotten that I would be texting and calling. Maybe Charvik the chauffeur didn't even talk to Flay. But then I thought, of *course* she's expecting me! I had put so much effort into finding a way out of my financial quagmire that I felt invincible. I sensed that the universal goddesses were on my side.

I had Flay *freaking* Tuber's personal phone number! I texted, *Hi Flay! Got UR # from Charvik the chauffeur. Would love 2 talk. May I call U?* To my glee and stupefaction, she texted back in less than three minutes. "In a meeting. Call me at 10:45." Of course she's in a meeting at 10:06 in the evening, right? High-powered, important, busy people were often in meetings. Then I wondered, did she mean call her at 10:45 this evening, as in thirty-nine minutes? Or 10:45 tomorrow morning? I didn't want to appear dim or indecisive, so I made the bold decision that she must have meant to call in thirty-nine minutes. My gut was right for once, and she answered.

"Hello. Flay here. Whatcha got?"

"Hello, Ms. Tuber. This is Goud Sugref. Charvik, your chauffeur, gave me your number and said it was all right to call."

"Oh, right! Charvik is quite a guy. Any friend of his is a potential headache of mine. Ha ha!" I chuckled, pleasantly surprised at her humor. "What's on your mind, Doug?"

I said, "Well, actually it's Goud, not Doug."

"Oops, sorry Goud. I'm dyslexic." I couldn't tell if she was joking or not. I decided to slip in a pun of mine I had been saving for years to use at just the right moment.

"Tell me, Flay, have you heard of the guy who was dyslexic, but every time he tried to say that word, it came out as 'lysdexic'?" There was a long pause. I was sure I had blown my chance to ask for a loan. My hope quickly drained away.

Then Flay burst out, "Goud! I almost choked on my rum and Coke! That was high-larious!" Phew! I was still in the game.

I replied, "I'm glad you liked it. Anyway, I'm calling you tonight to ask if you'd consider helping out a talented and charming young music group that I'm representing. We've made some great progress up the music business ladder, but we need some financial help to push us over the top." I went on to describe the situation in greater detail and then made the ask for the loan payback.

"*Six hundred thousand dollars?!*" Ms. Tuber shouted into the phone. I had mentally prepared myself for that possible reaction, but still, my confidence quickly capsized.

"I know, Flay! I realize it's no small potatoes."

"Oh, so you're making these puns a habit?"

"Yeah, I kinda can't help it."

"Well, I can help you by inserting my fist into your pie cavity, so please stop trying to be funny!" There was a leaden pause, then, "Only kidding, Goud-er-eeno!" I was on Flay's rollercoaster ride, just trying to hang on long enough to get the cash.

"I'm sorry to ask for the cash, but I think you'll see that this group really has great potential."

Another uncomfortably long pause, then, "All right Doug—I mean Goud. I want to see the group and hear them perform. Do you have a private place for them to play for me?"

"Yes! They live in a basement studio downtown. When do you want to see them?"

"How about twelve thirty."

"Okay, Flay. Twelve thirty tomorrow. We'll be ready for you!"

"No, Goud. Twelve thirty *tonight*. In about two hours. I'm a high-powered, very important, extremely busy, manic achiever. I can't wait fourteen hours to see this amazing band of yours!"

I jumped up. "Of course! I get it! Thank you! I'll text you the address. See you soon. I really appreciate this, Flay!"

Suddenly her tone turned cold, and she said in an almost evil whisper, "One more thing, Goud. *Never, ever* use my first name. Call me Ms. Tuber *only*." I froze, in fear again of losing this opportunity.

"Okay, Ms. Tuber. I, I understand."

"Ha! Gotcha, Goud! Only kidding! See you at twelve thirty."

* * *

In a panic, I hurriedly tapped out and sent a text to Matilda. *RU io? het band tigrther.bid delk!!!*
She responded, *Huh???*
I called her. "Sorry, I can't type quickly."
"You haven't been practicing the two-thumbs method that I showed you?"
"No, sorry, I haven't. I still use the hunt-and-peck method. I'm over thirty, remember? But no time for small talk! We have to audition for a financial backer in two hours!"
"What?! Oh, crap!" I had never heard Matilda curse. It made her seem even more charming and delightful. She pressed, "What kind of idiot wants to see a band at twelve thirty at night with no advance notice?"
I shouted, "Flay *freaking* Tuber! That's the idiot who wants to see you!"
"Oh wow and holy cow!" Matilda yelled.
I demanded, "Tell the others to get it together *now*! I'll be there as soon as I can. Rehearse only your three best songs. You know, like, 'Beards Are People Too,' and, ummm, 'The Smell of a Bluegrass Hippie,' and maybe..."
Matilda cut in and offered, "'Dontcha Wanna Touch My Hairy Legs?!'"
I yelped. "Yes! Great choice. See you soon!"
I hurriedly took a shower, then dressed in my

best-but-still-casual clothes. I wanted to smell and look like a powerhouse manager, worthy of investing in me and the Bushy Brown Beards. At the same time, I didn't want to overdress and appear slick and phony.

As a business professional herself, Flay would appreciate my attempting a good first impression. Asking for $600,000 was not a low-calorie, cholesterol-free request.

I dashed out the door of my apartment and ran along the covered outdoor walkway to the hazardously dark stairwell. I quickly stumbled down the corroded, cracked, flaking concrete steps to the sidewalk below. I hoofed it three blocks over to the Bushy Brown Beards' basement. As I approached, I heard them practicing my favorite song of theirs, "The Smell of a Bluegrass Hippie." I had written it for them after attending the Telluride Bluegrass Festival, where the air was continuously filled with the fumes of Mary-do-you-wanna, vegan lentil burritos, and the odor of bodies that likely hadn't seen water or soap for at least two weeks.

When I entered the basement, the band stopped playing. I told them, "You guys sound really good! No, not really good. Great! I think we're going to knock Ms. Tuber's socks off."

Matilda wrinkled her nose and said, "What does that mean?"

I asked her, "You've never heard that term?"

"Nope."

"Oh, right. Not only were you not yet born in the 1970s, when Steve Miller sang that line in 'True Fine Love,' but you weren't even alive in the '90s. You probably don't remember the Clinton/Lewinski scandal."

She said, "Oh, yeah, I remember that band. My friend's older brother had the first Clinton/Lewinski Scandal album."

I said, "Never mind. Let's kick the pants right off Flay Tuber's cute behind!"

"Ooh, that sounds like fun!" came a voice from the doorway.

"Oh, shit! Sorry, Ms. Tuber, I was—"

She cut me off. "I get it, Goud! I admire you for wanting the band's music to kick my pants off, ha ha!"

"Okay Flay—I mean Ms. Tuber. Please take a seat. Here are the Bushy Brown Beards! Take it away, band!"

The four of them poured their hearts and souls into the three songs they had rehearsed. After each song, Flay applauded heartily and whistled her approval, which really spurred on the band. After the last song, she stood up clapping and yelling, "Whoo-hoo!"

I stood, faced Flay, and smiled. "Tell us what you think, Ms. Tuber. Are they one of the best bands you've heard lately?!"

She looked pleased but not overly excited, and began her analysis. "Here is what I see. The music is certainly good, and the band plays well together. You are all youthful, energetic, and attractive. Well, *four* of you are. Ha! (She winked at me.) Let me look at you all. Hmmm. Okay, okay, looks good. Now turn around. Good. Let me see your smiles. Good. Well, Goudie old boy, here's my proppy-zition." I could hardly contain myself. I felt the incredible positive energy as if the whole world was going to open up to me and the band. "I won't loan you the money unless you redirect your energy away from trying to succeed in the music business and focus on being the stars that I know you all could be—and *will be*— in the *food* business." My heart dropped. I couldn't be sure if that was one of her quirky outbursts or if she was serious.

"Come on, guys," she continued. "You know that the odds are way stacked against you. In truth, you are as good as ten thousand other bands trying to make it right now. But of those ten thousand other bands, I think you guys are probably the most attractive in a bright, healthy way. You obviously have great nutritional awareness and eating habits."

All four members looked over at me as I smiled smugly. Matilda winked at me. Her eyes said, *Thank you for feeding us those horrible smoothies.*

"I want to hire all of you to work in my restaurant business and introduce you to the public via my new cooking show, 'Flay Will Slay You in the Kitchen.'" The four Bushy Brown Beards looked at me as if searching for a response to Flay's statement at the same moment that I looked over at them, hoping for the same thing.

* * *

"Welcome to The Lusty Russet!" said a bright-eyed Matilda in her cute, perky voice.

"How many in your party?" asked Jerezikial with a gleaming, toothpaste-commercial smile. The two best-looking members of the now-defunct Bushy Brown

Beards were a dual host-and-hostess team at the bustling Beverly Hills, California, flagship restaurant. They were so attractive and fun working together that they had become a hot topic in gossip circles and on social media. I, on the other hand, along with two remaining BBBs, were assigned to the kitchen. Flay learned about my unique self-taught cooking skills and steered me into the position of head chef and kitchen manager.

It has been over a year since that fateful meeting with her in the basement when she offered to pay off my $600,000 loan. She was keenly perceptive when she quickly surmised that the group (and me included) would do better in the restaurant/food business instead of continuing to toil in the music business, although I must say that we *did* have a success with music!

After putting Matilda and Jerezikial on her cooking show, the ratings rocketed the program up to number one within a month of their cute, fun, lively, moderately sexy appearance. Jerezikial then approached the other three BBBs and suggested they write an instrumental theme song for the show. When they presented it to Flay, she loved it and had it placed at the beginning and end of each episode. I released it as a single and had our old friend Wazlcpeoh promote it.

At the time of this writing, the theme song has had 427 million streams, which resulted in a payout of $1.708 million! But Wazlcpeoh spent $1,608 million on his sneaky, semi-legal tactics to generate the $1,708 million. Oh well, so what if we spent over a half mil to make a hunny grand? Not bad, right?

The big news is that we paid Flay back the six hunnerd K! We are now collectively bringing in a six-figure monthly paycheck. I still deposit all the money in the Overcooked Broccoli, LLC, bank account and keep my four cash cows on a salary. But now, instead of paying them fifty dollars a week, I pay them a whopping five hundred dollars every seven days. They don't actually know how much we earn, and I think it's best that way. I have the bulk of the money in various plans and investments, like on-shore tax huts and a company in Cabarete, Dominican Republic, that is developing a system of paving dirt roads in first, second, and third-world countries with olive pits.

Flay insisted I keep the BBBs on my special food plan. "Don't fix what ain't broke!" she exclaimed in regard to the diet that keeps them young, vibrant, and healthy-looking. To acknowledge Matilda's request for something that tastes better, I added vanilla extract to their wheat milk, tofu, powdered quail kidney, lima bean protein shakes.

The End

HOW TO HANDLE SEVERAL TALENTS

Here I am, trying to remain in the present tense. I tell myself, please don't write went if the appropriate words might be, go or goes. My delightful and wonderfully helpful wife, Suzan, told me, "Stay in your corner of the tense." But I *am* tense, and I can't write well when I'm not relaxed. Am I the only person on the planet who feels that it's unfair to curb my creative time? I have to squeeze in writing sessions throughout the day and night, in between other, more important life occurrences.

My typical schedule: Early morning before others in the house get up. Late at night after others have gone to bed. Sitting in my car during my half-hour lunch breaks down at the factory. (Have you ever noticed that factories are never *up* from any place? They are only *down*. Never have I heard or seen a sentence such as, "I work *up* at the factory." Imagine how weird it would sound if that wonderful country song by Kenny Rogers called "The Factory" had the line, "And thank you, Lord, for my job *up* at the factory.")

Years ago, I paid for test results that proved my IQ was at a genius level. Is that not enough proof? Sheesh-a-Maria! Geniuses need love, too. When I applied for my current job as a *debris vessel manipulation specialist* up at the Hunt Wesson tomato processing plant, (I've since been promoted to a level 1 apprentice! I'm allowed to carry tools and when asked, hand them to the lead technician!) I wrote *Genius IQ* in the space for *highest level of education*.. I'm sure the management was intimidated by my boundless, colossal knowledge of the job to which I was applying. Sure, it scared them to allow me into their world. But it was the best decision they had ever made. Am I riiiigggghhht?

I know I should check my attitude, and I hear you when you say, "Have you read any self-help books lately?" Heck-a-Maria, no I have *not* read any frickin' self-help books lately! But seriously, if I didn't have to work up at this darn factory, I might have time to write one.

So, um, basically (ha ha, I'm teasing you, reader; we both know to *never* start a sentence with *so*, *um*, or *basically*; am I riiiigghhht?), I was sitting in my car in the parking lot of the Hunt Wesson factory, waiting for my shift to start at seven one morning. I have to leave my house at 5:45 so that I avoid the heavy traffic on the freeway. That gets me to the factory about twenty minutes early.

I rested for a few minutes before strolling over to the time clock. As I stared into amplitudes of the oxygenated troposphere and nibbled on a Lenny and Larry's snickerdoodle cookie, I saw a school bus go by on the road outside the factory compound. Then I thought of all the children on the bus and hoped some of them would become full-time writers instead of debris vessel manipulation specialists. But that's what we *real* writers do, don't we? We ponder societal quandaries, contemplate linguistic methodologies, and use italics.

Gene Simmons, the bassist in the rock band Kiss, said that he really admires writers who toil away for hours a day instead of waiting around for inspiration to strike. "It's 99 percent perspiration and 1 percent inspiration," he said. We writers can't help it; we live and breathe writing. But some of us also have to deal with many other thoughts that occupy our heads. We aren't the lucky ones who *only* write. We mentally juggle multiple stresses during the frenetic commute to our freaking—I mean *lovely*—day job, where we must be mentally sharp as we maintain the machinery that converts tomatoes to sauce.

Sometimes I'll be in the break room, thinking of a great line for a story I'm working on, when suddenly Betty from the production floor will call on my two-way radio. "Hey, Dougie dipstick! The Manwich mixer paddle on tank 3 stopped again. I think it's a blown fuse." I have to refrain from telling her she's wrong, that it's not the freakin' fuse. I employ my superior human relations skill set and choose to say, "Thanks, Betty! It's nice of you to let me know about tank 3. I'll look into it right away."

The truth is, she can't know what is wrong with the mixer paddle, and she's trying to stray out of her area of expertise. I say to myself, *Betty. You are a wonderful lead person on your shift. You are a nice, sweet, loving mom, a fantastic organizer of activities for your kids. You are a whiz at Trivial Pursuit and can do eight pull-ups, twenty-five pushups, and squat 185 pounds at your local CrossFit class. I'm sure your husband adores you and your banana bread is so good that if I were lost on safari, crawling across the desert with no water, I would keep going with the thought of tasting a slice of your almond flour, banana, carob chips, goji berries, pulverized soy bean, and diet cola baked treat when I was finally rescued. But you don't know a thing about the Manwich mixer on tank 3!*

It's not fair that I have to write on my lunch half-hour at work, is it? Other people have it easy. They pick one job (or stumble upon one job), and that's it. They do it their whole lives until they get old and quit and then live out their days in south Sacramento in a deluxe Fleetwood mobile home with a Coleman furnace in a mobile home park covered with gravel and concrete until they croak.

One of my coworkers here at the Hunt Wesson tomato processing plant has it the easiest of all. His passion and reason for being is to watch as many old black-and-white 1950s and '60s television shows as he possibly can before he rides off to the big tomato in the sky. He watches early in the morning before work. He watches on the break room TV at lunch. (Don't dare even suggest to him that he change the channel to a different program!) He talks all day about the various programs he'll watch when he gets home after work. I envy him. His passion and purpose are clear, and he's living and achieving his goals constantly. Even though I talk the big talk of being a writer, I can't deny that I was born a mechanical genius with wrenches and screwdrivers floating along in my veins. I ain't no phony when it comes to maintenance! We *real* maintenance workers are a different breed of cat, cow, and canary. I wouldn't say we were *born* to do maintenance, because we are gifted in many mechanical areas. The thing that separates us from skilled workers who do only *one* task is that we have a fear of not being good enough to be called an *expert* at one thing, so we get *pretty good* at many things, then allow our inferiority complexes to kick in before we reach the level of expert. Skilled maintenance *engineers* (that's us!) are required to have personal relations skills *and* technical skills.

So, I can't tell Betty that she's a stupid, diet-cola-guzzling ignoramus for telling me that the reason the Manwich mixer paddle stopped is because of a blown fuse. It takes great restraint, patience, and a kindness-is-my-religion attitude to not tell her to shut the %$^&# up and let me do my job. How could she know anything about a Manwich mixer? I took a whole *eight-hour* class to learn the elaborate intricacies and staggeringly complex stuff about them. She is indeed smart enough to be the swing-shift lead worker. And she, too, has to juggle all her skills as she makes her way through life. But as I mentioned previously, maybe her greatest gift is her yummy bread. I've heard she adores her spouse and child. At the company picnic three years ago, she slayed everyone at the trivia contest, but she ain't no Manwich mixer troubleshooter!

Oh sure, many people do more than one activity in their lives, but they *dabble*. I detest the label of dabbler. In my mind's eyeball, I have to try to be great at everything I do. In trying to be great, I feel that I rise above the dabbler and become one who is in the same *category* as an expert. I certainly *could* be a professional. Couldn't we all? I know that I'm good enough to become a legit, full-time writer, because the great author Earnjohn Hemingbeck himself told me as much at his writing workshop last year. (It was very affordable. Only twelve payments of $1,299.99.)

Gosh darn it! I can't be *just* a great maintenance worker at this Hunt-Wesson tomato processing plant. How about you, lovely reader? What is your greatest gift and reason for being? Speaking of me, have I told you already that I have to be a great writer in addition to my other gifts? Oh. I *have* already told you several times? All right, but my value on this planet depends upon me continuing to pursue that goal. And it's not a *dream*, it's a *goal*, dammit!

I'm driven from some internal place, or maybe a place in the cosmos. I may need the great boxer and astrophysicist Mike deGrasse Tyson to explain that to me. Where do I focus my energy? I'm convinced that I've been given several skills-slash-gifts to test me and make me continue relentlessly toward my main purpose. Just like bears who can lift great weights, it's a great weight to bear, isn't it?

Would you consider it a gift or a handicap that I'm a good kisser? What about my ability to skillfully true bicycle and motorcycle wheels? Certainly, I'm the best wheel truer in my county. I bet I'm the best kisser on my block. Am I the best maintenance man at the Hunt

Wesson tomato processing plant? Ha, no contest! Then there is also normal life stuff, like being the best husband and father, right? Can I be the best husband-slash-father-slash-kisser-slash-wheel truer-slash-maintenance man *and* be a prize-winning author? Sheesh-a-Maria, I hope so!

GOOD AT TOO MANY THINGS

My problem is that I'm good at anything I try. You too? How do we choose which *one* thing to pursue? Sheesh-a-Maria!

My neighbor has a great-step-aunt who was a free agent for the Omaha Spiny Lumpsuckers professional tetherball team. That sounds like a cool job, but I want to be paid, right? Wouldn't you? Free agent my eye! I would demand to be, at minimum, a 50 percent-off agent.

I currently have a roommate who used to work for a top-selling kitty litter factory. She was highly paid as an anti-clumping agent. Then one day she was approached by an evil competing kitty litter company. The evil company wanted to infuse some chaos that would create a toppling effect and eventually put the leading company out of business. My roommate took the offer and became an anti-clumping agent provocateur.

Associate Professor

I'd love to be an associate professor at a college. Wouldn't we all? Not just a plain run-of-the-mill professor, mind you. An *associate* professor. It has a ring of intelligence to it. "Hello, Associate Professor Sugref? We cordially invite you to give the keynote speech at the 2023 ASCABBU (Accelerated Strategic Confluence of Artificial Bubble Bath Users) conference at Stanchevy University."

But then my day fantasy burst as I remembered the bummer. Even associate professors need a degree. Isn't there a quicker way? Certificate courses online? *Become an associate professor in two weeks! Do it in the privacy and stinky slovenliness of your bedroom!* No? Drat, Jim!

Massive Bonus

I want a job where I get a massive bonus every year. I'd negotiate it and demand it and I'd get it because I'm the smartest person in the room (well, my bathroom). How about a massive bonus every month or every week? Shoot, let's have a massive hourly bonus! If I worked in an office as a tremendously sought-after message writer, maybe I could demand a massive missive bonus!

Cooking School

Fine reader, would you like to start a cooking school with me? Our new gastronomical academy would feature only fare that contains a bright yellow chemical produced by plants of the *Curcuma longa* species. Our website would proudly proclaim that our school has a *curcumin curriculum*.

Media Baron

Do media barons make good money? I like the sound of

it. Let's say it together, slowly: m e d i a b a r o n. Would I need a college degree, or is there a mail-order class where I could get my Media Baron certificate? When I was discussing this matter with my adorable friend Laneisha one day, she told me I should also look into being a media proprietor, a media tycoon, or a media mogul.

She said, "You know, Goud, if you were a big player in the TV and movie business and liked to snow ski down bumpy slopes, you might be a media mogul mogul skier."

"Very funny, Laneisha. Did you know that there are many snow-covered bumpy slopes in the area surrounding Los Angeles?"

"I did not know that, Goud. Tell me about it."

"Haven't you heard of Hollywood moguls?"

"Oh, Goud. Will you be here entertaining us all week, or just one night?"

"Oh, Laneisha, I love your encouragement, but I need to get a move-on if I'm going to become a mover and shaker in media."

"Here's an idea," she offered. "If you can't find work as a media baron, tycoon, or mogul, there is another option for you to enter the media field."

I perked up. "Really? Tell me about it!"

"You could be a *disgraced* media baron."

"Of course! Thanks for that tip, Laneisha! I'll check into it."

In truth, I don't think I could become a disgraced media baron. My research tells me that it requires doing something repugnant, abhorrent, or execrable. That's just not in my wheelhouse. (And yes, Repugnant, Abhorrent and Execrable is the law firm that represented several disgraced media barons.)

In reality (don't tell Laneisha), I didn't even try to become a media baron. It sounded too complicated. (Although at five foot seven and 135 pounds I might qualify to be a medium baron.)

I told Laneisha, "I scoured Zip Recruiter, LinkedIn, and the Craigslist Help Wanted section and didn't see anything that interested me until my eyes popped at *Hedge Fund Manager*. Hmmm. I'm pretty sure I could do that!"

"If you work hard and pay attention," she deadpanned, "you might get promoted to Hedge Fund Billionaire."

"Maybe I should first focus on being a hedge *trimmer* manager, then work my way up to hedge trimmer billionaire?" I asked.

"And if that doesn't work out," she retorted, "you could always have a fine career as a *hedgehog* manager."

Global Head

I'd like to be the global head of something. I'd like to have a job where I don't get dirt under my fingernails or toenails. Do global heads stay clean on the job? I think so. I think I'll have GLOBAL HEAD emblazoned on my business cards and letterhead. (Am I the only person who thinks the word *emblazoned* should mean *to set on fire*? The secret agent's supervisor congratulated the secret agent after he *emblazoned* the mob boss's car.) Maybe my business card would read:

GLOBAL HEAD
Global Head of Product Management for Gluing Noodles to Cardboard in the Shape of a Giraffe
Eastern Octasphere
World

In truth, I'd like to find a job where I'm global head of Rubbing My Tummy, Patting My Head, and Burping "The Star-Spangled Banner." If not a global head, maybe I could be a *regional* head. Like, Regional Head of Slippers, Sandals, Staplers, Sinks, and Sleds for Scalability Institutions, Asia Pacific, Singapore.

Financial Advisor

I'm not very good with money in my personal life, but I'm decidedly adept at telling people what to do with theirs. I wonder if there is a fast-track online course to earn my certificate in financial advising. I'd like to be an ally for the lower classes and advise them in the ubiquitous Bear Stearns high-grade structured credit strategies and enhanced leverage hedge funds. (*Enhanced leverage* is where you put a piece of pipe over the handle of your lug wrench, making it longer so that it's easier to take the lug nuts off your car wheel.)

I would explain to my garbage collecting, ditch-digging and sheetrock-installing clients that "this fund contains six altitudinous convergences with a moderate ascendancy quotient in swindle-backed, collateralized debt obligations." I would occasionally need to feel superior to them and exhale loudly with frustrated haughtiness, "Okay. One. More. Time. What part of *high-grade structured corroborated hedge-enhanced strategies* don't you understand?"

Phone Book College

Laneisha revealed to me that she had attended a phone book college in upstate Utah. It was intended to be a Bible college, but the founders couldn't agree on which religion to base the curriculum. At a board of directors meeting, a huge argument erupted. A man stood up and vociferated ironically, "All right, then! Let's base our course of study on the damn phone book!" The rest of the board liked the idea. It was voted on and passed unanimously.

Laneisha explained, "In order to have enough textbooks, the students were required to walk door to door and ask people to give them the phone books that the phone company leaves on everyone's doorstep. As you know, in this modern cell phone and computer age, no one uses them anymore."

I asked, "Did you also go to recycling drop-off centers and dumpster dive to retrieve more of the thick yellow directories?"

"Why, yes, we did!" she exclaimed. "The students were required to pick their major by closing their eyes, opening the phone book to a random page, circling their index finger round and round, then stabbing the page. Wherever their finger landed, that's what they had to study."

"That's weird and wacky!" I declared as I took a bite of my eclair.

"It sure was! My finger landed on Oat Fiber Napkin Design Management and Consulting."

"But you don't work in that field anymore, right?"

She frowned. "I hated it. But I actually loved my early college days of gathering phone books, talking to people, and walking through neighborhoods, so I quit and started my own wildly successful business selling 'No Soliciting' signs door to door."

I jumped up. "And that's how we met! I bought one of your signs on my doorstep. I cherish that day!"

She lowered her head slightly and said, "Aw shucks-a-reen-o, Goud."

THIS PAGE WAS ACCIDENTALLY LEFT BLANK

Break Time

Union rules dictate that we must take a break. Please enjoy the following advertisement from our staggeringly supportive and sensational sponsor, Bumpkins Shovel Holding and Leaning Academy:

> Hello, I'm an instructor here at the Bumpkins Shovel Holding and Leaning Academy. We are a direct pipeline to the human resources departments at all major city and county roads and highway repair agencies. We also represent privately owned excavating, ditch-digging, and road repair companies. Once you graduate from our course, we guarantee you'll get an interview. Learn how to properly stand and lean on a shovel so that you don't look like a rookie. Learn how to shoot the breeze using the right blend of profanity and slang so that you don't appear as an outsider.
>
> We'll teach you how to hold and smoke a cigarette without inhaling so that you look cool but won't get lung disease. You'll learn to chew tobacco and spit so your coworkers will know you're legit. We'll train you to skillfully deliver dirty jokes and to laugh convincingly at your coworkers' stupid and politically incorrect jokes so that you fit right in.
>
> Call today and we'll throw in, Farting on Command at no additional cost!

BILL Talks

I would like to be in demand as a speaker and give dozens of commencement speeches and TED Talks. Heck, I'd even like to give a lot of BILL Talks. I would give talks about one of my major talents: the ability to make the sound of a Honda 175 four-stroke motorcycle engine revving and gears shifting. If you have a compatible talent, you could act out, mime-style, a person riding a motorcycle. We could entertain people at that famous outdoor walkway Las Ramblas in Barcelona. Of course, I'm talking about the Las Ramblas in Barcelona, Kentucky. We could practice and refine our act until we couldn't be ignored. Soon, both Hollywood and the internet would come calling for a piece of us. Eventually, everyone would want to know our back story. We might even BILL Talks as a team.

We would have our manager negotiate ridiculously high, never-before-seen fees for our public appearances. We would become so in demand that we would eventually put a note on our website: "(Your name here) no longer gives public performances for any amount of money." As the decades moved along, we would receive dozens of requests for those where-are-they-now TV shows.

We would instruct our manager to approve only one interview per five-year period, and it still would perturb us to no end. We would retire and spend the rest of our lives in the garden of our 26,000-acre English country estate. You would spend hours each day pruning the delphiniums with tiny scissors from a travel sewing kit. I would sit in repose, watching you snip while I sip Duke Gray tea and softly strum delicious and dreamy chords on my twelfth-century lute.

Please Buy My Baskets

When I'm not looking for a day job, writing, playing bass guitar, or coveting an exotic motorcycle, I'm probably weaving a basket. But I'm not a corporate-sponsored basket-braider, so I need you to support me. Please buy my baskets. How am I supposed to pay for the basket-shaped pool I'm having installed in my backyard if you don't buy them? Would it help your decision to purchase my baskets if I tell you I use only fresh, organic, fair-trade willow? Well, I do! I also sing sweet, sappy-but-encouraging lullabies to my willow branches as they grow and just before I chop them off the tree.

You might yell at me with a resentful, jealous, provocative tone, "Hey author-wannabe Dougie dipstick! Why don't you use your music streaming or book royalties to pay for the basket-shaped pool?!"

Well, dear reader, I can't use my music or book royalties because *those* are being spent on the guitar-shaped motorcycle I'm having custom-built.

Some Don't Like Chocolate

This piece is not about looking for a day job, but my editor let me keep it in because she doesn't like chocolate.

Did you know that there are people in the world who don't like the taste of chocolate? They are living in a society where 99 percent of people *love* chocolate. Chocolate mentally hurts the people who don't like chocolate, and they're suffering because they feel spurned.

(I bet none of my friends will repost this on Facebook or send it out to every one of their email contacts. To prove you're a real friend of mine, and if you care about people who don't like chocolate, email this to all your contacts, including me, then repost it on your Facebook page and send it back to me within ten minutes. I bet I know which of my friends won't do it. I'll spend an entire day carefully scouring my list of 768 friends and all my email contacts, noting which ones didn't repost, then gleefully unfriend and/or delete each one of them.)

And now a word from yet another sponsor:

PROFESSIONAL DOODLERS NEEDED!

Top pay and benefits! Flexible hours, work-from-home options. We provide a ballpoint pen and a spiral notebook. Please be proficient at depicting funny faces of teachers and classmates and drawing curlicues, three-dimensional-looking boxes, and ever-expanding grids of triangles (with every other triangle filled in by dense, quick scribbling, not caring if some lines go across into the unscribbled triangle.)

Bonuses for those who can draw a flower around each of the three holes in the vertical margin.

Handlers

Some famous humans on the planet have *handlers*. It seems weird to me that any human would need to have a handler. I'd love to be so important that I would need to have a handler. Or better yet, I could *be* a handler. If I were feeling kinda naughty, I might want to be handled by a handler. I would want to listen to the music of Handel while being handled by a handler. I wonder if comedienne Chelsea Handler needs a handler. If she employs two handlers, and I could be one of them, maybe I could be handled by Chelsea Handler's handler while I'm handling Chelsea Handler.

Anchor People

Aren't you astounded at all the different ways people earn a living? Let's imagine a world where all news and morning show anchors are a team consisting of a woman who is over sixty-five and a goofy male sidekick who is under twenty-five. The people of the world have become sick of seeing gorgeous faces. In this new world, the networks will not allow beautiful people to be on air, leading to hundreds of hopeful, pulchritudinous actors and models getting plastic surgery to make themselves look average so they can get work. The ALPU (Average-Looking People's Union) would become the most powerful union in Hollywood. And I would have an advantage if I applied for an anchor position because I wouldn't have any telltale scars.

Don't Quit Your Night Job

Most musicians I know work at night and sleep during the day, so you can't tease them and yell, "Don't quit your day job!" You have to yell, "Don't quit your night job!" Here's the lyrics to a song I wrote about it:

DON'T QUIT YOUR NIGHT JOB

Rolling down the highway on to another town.
Get up on the stage, act like a freaking clown.
Living in the van, where am I supposed to take a crap?
Hurry hurry up, when can I take a nap?
Don't quit your night job

Oh wee oh oh

Don't quit tonight

Na na na na na na

What else can I do in order to stay in one place?

Supermarket checker, dig a ditch, wash a plate?

My drummer looks at me and says are you out of your mind?

The only thing we know is doing this night club grind

Don't quit your night job

Oh wee oh oh

Don't quit tonight

Na na na na na na

Hey there little dreamer floating out there in space

Stick to what you know plucking your four string bass

Whatcha gonna do now, learn a new trade by mail?

Be a rocket surgeon, fix a car, pound a nail?

Don't quit your night job

Oh wee oh oh

Don't quit tonight

Na na na na na na

(Find this song and many others by Lucky Doug Fergus on your favorite digital platform.)

I'M GOING TO MAKE IT!
(I THINK)

My name is Kirsten Kristen-Kiersten. In my parents' generation, hyphenating names became fashionable. Parents were even changing their last names to create monikers for their children comprising three similar names, usually hyphenating the last two. I was born to parents who thought it would be cute and clever to name their kids following this new trend. They were two of the first parents to name their children this way. This is why my name is Kirsten Kristen-Kiersten. They also adopted an adorable boy, my brother, Tim Todd-Ted.

I'm an actress and wannabe comedian. One day I was driving along the 605 Freeway through Whittier on my way to an audition. Tim was riding along for moral support and to get a taste of the audition process since his dream was to be a professional dancer. We motored along, like Sister Christian, toward the audition in Burbank, the famous home of NBC television in California.

"Hey, Tim, isn't it interesting that some people have

two names that sound exactly the same but are spelled differently?"

"Yes!" he agreed. "I think you're referring to the famous talk show personality Baylee Baighleigh."

"That's right. I hope to someday be a guest on her show. I would ask her, 'Are you listed in the phone book as Baighleigh-comma-Baylee'?"

Tim shook his head. "Not funny. Don't do it."

"Oh, Tim, why stifle my creative flow? Roll with me."

"I'll start rolling with you when you get new tires on your joke-mobile."

Baylee Baighleigh's life partner was the celebrated androgynous actor Aliyah Alan-Ainsley. Everyone loves Aliyah's movies. All types of people are attracted to the way Aliyah walks and talks. They yearn to be in Aliyah's safe, fun, inviting presence. And that smile! Looking at that fetching, fabulous face could cure one of a disease. It didn't hurt that Aliyah had a wide jaw containing several more teeth than the average human possesses. Hollywood dentists made no money off them because each incisor, canine, and molar was as straight as a Wyoming cowboy and as genetically white as new-fallen St. Moritz snow.

After a long silence, I said, "Did you know that in England there are places where automobiles go to play Frisbee, make drug deals, fly kites, and have picnics?"

"Gosh, Kirsten, really?"

"Yes, Tim. Over there, they have *car parks*!"

Tim sat there, poker faced. "All right," he finally responded. "It's not actually funny, but I wouldn't toss it in the trash. Yet."

"Thanks. Text it to me so I don't forget it."

"You didn't recite that from memory? You just improvised that?"

"Yes. Quick! Text it to me or it'll evaporate!" "All right, all right, corral your ponies." He tapped out, *In England. Places 4 autos 2 play Frisbee, make deals, kites, picnics. Car parks.* His phone made a *whoosh* sound. "Text sent."

* * *

We drove along the 605 to the 289, took the 351 for a few miles, cloverleafed onto the 409, hopped onto the 454 to get to the 80, then over to the 125, down to the 250, and finally brapped onto the 500. I took the N. Buena Vista St. offramp and—no, I didn't literally *take* the offramp; where would I put it? Hang it on my living room wall?—navigated three right turns through beautiful downtown Burbank, made a left, and steered into the parking lot.

I thought I'd take this opportunity to tell you a bit about my car. It's a 1986 Oldsmobile Calais Supreme. Why did they call it *supreme*, as if it's a burrito with extra cheese and pineapple-cantaloupe salsa? And what is a *calais* anyway? I Googled it. It's a city in France, a city in the state of Maine, and a city in the state of Vermont. Ooh, and there's a professional football player named Calais Campbell. He's six-foot-eight and weighs three hundred pounds. Hmmm. I'm beginning to like the name of my car better now. It's primer gray and primer red and has endured over four hundred thousand miles.

Over the course of the three and a half decades since my Calais Supreme rolled out of the factory, five different teens and young adults had their first humping-like-a-couple-of-crazed-camels experience in the back seat, front seats, on the hood, and even in the trunk of the car. Over the decades, all four corners had been crunched by various owners who used the I-don't-care-if-there-isn't-enough-room-between-those-cars method of parking. The interior has a permanent fragrance of that famous cologne College Boys Dorm Room, with a splash of that other famous cologne, Dark Smokey Boozy Nightclub Where Fornicating Is Allowed In The Back Booths. I can barely stand the awful stench, but in my price range for a car, it's either going to be a pile of crap that breaks down constantly, is beat up like a sixty-year-old boxer, or has an aroma like the inside of a frat boys' TV and game room. Fortunately for me, the Calais Supreme has never left me stranded out on the road.

I parked the car, got out, and paraded across the asphalt to a wide steel door with "Explosives – What Were You Expecting?" stenciled across it. Tim trailed me in an emotionally supportive, maybe-I-could-someday-be-your-boyfriend sort of way. But, being my brother, it was more like a maybe-I-could-someday-be-your-boyfriend-but-darn it-I'm-your-brother sort of way.

"Not too fast, Kirsten!" he yelled. "Wait for me! There's something creepy about this building!"

I looked over my shoulder and yelled back, "There's something creepy about every building where auditions are held, especially in LA!"

At the door, I aggressively grabbed the knob. (Is that a British slang sexual reference?)

Tim said, "Shouldn't you knock first?"

I ignored him, and with a mighty twist of the knob (ha!) I pushed the door open and confidently stepped in with Tim in tow. After driving in the intense Southern California sun, we both had to stand motionless for a few seconds, letting our eyes adjust to the dimly lit space. We were in a gigantic warehouse-type building as big as fifty tennis fields or twenty basketball rinks or ten football diamonds or thirty hockey courts. It was crammed with hundreds of antique furnaces and air conditioners.

Way over in one corner was a workshop area, where a hunched-over figure was tink-tap-tap tink-tap-tapping with a hammer on something metal. We later found out this was a full-time worker who restored and maintained the fleet of heating and cooling machines. His responsibilities included starting up each furnace and air conditioner once a month to keep all the moving parts from falling into stagnation.

Suddenly a door burst open. A tall figure quickly walked through and waved in our direction. "Hello!" boomed the tall figure. "If you're here to see the furnace and A/C museum, clap twice. If you're here for the audition, clap four times and say 'toodle-do' in falsetto."

When the figure finally appeared close enough to be recognizable, my mouth dropped open and Tim gasped in delight. We both squealed in all caps, "OMG! It's Aliyah Alan-Ainsley in real life!"

They/them greeted us with that patented gorgeous smile and a fist bump. Tim was starstruck and couldn't speak, but he scanned the room and motioned with his hand at all the heating, ventilating, and air conditioning equipment—HVAC. Aliyah said, "Ah, yes. You're curious about all these glorious old furnaces and A/C units, aren't you?"

I said, "Yes, he is, and so am I."

Tim had gathered his nerves enough to ask, "I figured maybe you were a guitar collector or a car fanatic, but never would I have guessed you were into all this."

"No cars for me," Aliyah said. "I leave the auto collecting to my friend and neighbor, Jay Leno. In fact, we share the same mechanic. That old codger back there in my workshop is Jay's top technician."

I looked over at Tim as we both smiled with the exact same thought bubble over our heads: *I can't believe I'm here in Aliyah's museum!* Suddenly Aliyah clapped their hands and said, "I believe you are here today to audition for the role of sidekick on my show. Am I right?"

I stammered, "N-n-n-no, um, well, yes, I think so?" My agent, Trixannie, had told me it was for a dog food TV commercial, not for the position of Aliyah's sidekick! I suppose she was protecting me from freaking out about the possibility of working on Aliyah's show. I stepped aside for a moment and let Aliyah and Tim talk. I texted Trixannie, *WTF? Dog Food Comm? Is this correct addy? Aliyah Alan-Ainsley is here!*

She responded, *:-)) Right! UR ready! Don't B nervous!*

I stepped back over to Aliyah and Tim. Aliyah was wide-eyed and excited. "I have a show coming out on the Stupid Waste of Precious Time channel called *Conversations and Decaf with Comedians while Staring at My*

Furnace and A/C Collection. It's going to be *fascinating!*"

Tim and I smiled and nodded our heads enthusiastically. Caught up in the moment, he blurted, "That sounds great! But doesn't Jerry Seinfeld already have a similar show?" Aliyah's excitement screeched to a halt. I threw Tim my best dagger eyes. Dang it! It's *my* audition! I hoped that Tim's thoughtless remark didn't quash my chance to be Aliyah's sidekick. Fortunately, he broke the silence. "Tell me, Aliyah, how did you develop this obsession with HVAC?" Thankfully, it seemed to pull Aliyah out of their funk.

"My grandmother was a theater actor, and my grandfather was a radio voice actor. My mother and father were both career regional theater actors. I didn't have the acting bug when I was growing up. I loved cars and motorcycles and science classes. In college, I took a class on thermodynamics and became hooked on the whole heating and cooling field.

"My parents made me promise to choose the safe path of acting if my first choice of being a heating and air tech fell through. After graduating from college and getting a job working for an HVAC company, I just couldn't get it. I tried and tried, but even though I was fascinated with the concept of HVAC, I finally had to admit that I didn't have an inherent talent in the actual practice. Depressed and feeling like a failure, I called my parents to tell them the news. They were relieved when I told them I was leaving HVAC for the acting world and that I was studying comedy at night in order to be a more well-rounded actor." Tim and I nodded to show concern and understanding.

Aliyah blurted, "I mean, HVAC is more complicated than most people know!" We sped up our head-nodding.

"Yes! We get it! You don't have to tell us!" I said.

Aliyah, clearly embarrassed to have quit HVAC, continued. "So, after trying for two years, I realized I needed to let the real HVAC techs take care of business. It was a tough decision to abandon my dream and become an actor."

I said, "I've only seen your dramatic work. Did you ever do stand-up or take any comedic roles?"

"I'm a closet comedian. It's my little secret. Now it's *our* little secret. May I tell you the first joke I ever wrote?"

I looked over at Tim as we said simultaneously, "Please do!"

Aliyah smiled proudly. "Why is a book of synonyms called a thesaurus? It should be called a synaurus or a book of thynonyms." Tim let out a polite guffaw. I was speechless at the thought that I was standing next to a bona fide celebrity who just told me the first joke they ever wrote.

I suddenly remembered the perfect follow-up for this exact moment. I had written a joke years before but hadn't had the opportunity to use it. I didn't want to upstage Aliyah and possibly ruin my chances to be their sidekick, but on the other hand, maybe this would let them know that I'm witty and worthy of being selected. "Hey, Aliyah, what about the word *lisp*?"

"What about it?"

"People with a lisp can't say the word *lisp*! That's just cruel!"

Tim turned away to hide his embarrassment and was fully expecting to be shot down for my amateurish attempt at humor. To my surprise, Aliyah smiled and winked at me. "Not bad."

*　*　*

"Anyway," Aliyah continued, "four years ago I was set to begin production on my show about having coffee with comedians while looking at my collection of furnaces and A/Cs. Then, out of thin air, that rat fink Seinfeld comes out with a show about comedians driving around in old cars getting coffee! So, I scrapped the idea. Get it? *Scrapped* the idea?" Tim started to giggle. I scrunched up my forehead and said, "No I don't get it." Aliyah smiled and with gesticulating hands said, "A show about furnaces and A/Cs? Furnaces and A/Cs are made of *metal*? *Scrapped* the idea? *Scrap* metal?"

I shook my head, smiled, and said, "Oh, scrap, I shoulda got that one!" Aliyah smiled at my play on words. There was a slightly uncomfortable silence, then I said, "Hey, Aliyah, I hope your career never tanks." We all burst out laughing. "*Tanked*. HA! I get it! Tanks are made of metal that someday get *scrapped*. Good one . . . uh, what's your name?"

"Kirsten Kristen-Kiersten. And this is my SMSSCMPS, Tim Todd-Ted."

Aliyah smiled and reached out to shake my hand. "Hello, Kirsten Kristen-Kiersten and, uh . . . what's an SMSSCMPS?"

"Sweet, mellow, sometimes slightly clingy, mildly protective sibling."

Aliyah smiled. "That's a funny way to describe him. Clever. Regarding the TV show, I told my producers and management that I wanted to go ahead with the show about comedians looking at furnaces and A/Cs and deal with any possible Seinfeld copyright infringement later. He's such a funny guy, he must be very nice in person, don't you think?" Tim and I both nodded our heads.

At this point, Aliyah asked us to go inside a small room and wait for my turn to audition. Tim and I complied, went into the room, sat on cheap plastic folding chairs, and waited for my name to be called. I was relaxed now, having already met the star of the show. I figured this might give me an advantage over the other auditionees. Someone eventually called my name.

The tryout was fun. I decided to test the waters of Aliyah's sense of humor with the joke I had just told Ted. "Did you know that in England there are places where automobiles go to play Frisbee, make drug deals, fly kites, and have picnics?"

Aliyah said, "Gosh, Kirsten, really?"

"Yes. Over there, they have *car parks*!" Polite smiles from the crew. A production assistant instructed me to carry on.

"My Uncle Letka, the research scientist, was always a little behind his peers. Instead of pushing the envelope, he was often *dragging* it." Aliyah's head tilted slightly, trying to detect something funny. Uh-oh. Maybe that one went out there too far. "I'm a little embarrassed to tell you that my Aunt Mirabel was a schizophrenic who drank too much. She developed psychosis of the liver." Aliyah chuckled at that one.

"All right, Kirsten. Not bad. Thank you. We'll be in touch." I left the building feeling elated that something good would come of this, even if I wasn't chosen to be Aliyah's sidekick.

Tim suggested we go celebrate at our favorite bar, All This Alcohol Will Become Urine In Two Hours. "Sure!" I enthused. "Our favorite British/country/punk band, Hank Buggeroff and the Prairie Wankers, goes on at midnight!"

* * *

Oldsmobile Faithful carried me and Tim the twelve miles from the audition in Burbank to the bar. Upon arriving, we were told that Hank Buggeroff and the Prairie Wankers would not be performing due to a blown hydraulic flywheel diode that left their tour bus stranded halfway between Blythe and Desert Center, California. Instead, there would be a comedian performing in a comedy room at the back of the building called The Dreaded Plateau.

At promptly eight o'clock a twenty-something man, five foot nine, average build, with a golden-brown goatee and a blue bowler on his head, stepped up to the microphone and hollered, "Hellooooo Pasadenaaaaa!" A few tipsy patrons hollered woo-hoo along with a smattering of claps. "I'm Justin Jason-Jeremy. How many of you here tonight like to play the game of cribbage?"

A few hands rose into the air, accompanied by a modicum of comments. "Me." "Yeah." "I love to!"

Justin replied, "I don't. I'd rather play a game of

cabbage." Nothing. No one responded. I couldn't decide if his joke was clever, stupid, or not a joke at all. Three seconds later I suddenly found it absurd and let a little chuckle slip out of my mouth. "Okay!" Justin said, looking directly at me. "We have one intelligent person in the house." I smiled back at him.

"All right then, who wants to play non-sports-follower *Jeopardy*?" Nobody answered him, so I timidly raised my hand to half-mast and said, "I do." He shot me a look, "All right, all right, all right. Here's the answer, young lady. 'How many baskets does it take to make a home run?'"

The audience was silent. I didn't know whether I should attempt a real answer or just improvise a silly comeback. I didn't want to embarrass Justin. I leaned over and whispered to Tim, "What should I say?" Tim whispered back, "What did the non-sports-follower say to the bartender?"

I shrugged my shoulders and said to Justin, "Will you repeat the answer, please?"

Justin replied, "Sure thing... uh... what's your name?" "Kirsten." "All right, Kirsten, 'How many baskets does it take to make a home run?'"

I looked at Tim for assurance as he nodded and whispered, "Just say it!"

I said, "What did the non-sports-follower say to the bartender?"

Justin's mouth fell open. "Ha! Wow. No one has ever answered that correctly." He made air quotes as he said *correctly*. He looked into my eyes for a couple of seconds as someone got up and walked out. I was feeling uneasy about how badly Justin was bombing, but I had a warm feeling that the two of us were riding on the same sine wave. I was starting to think he could be clever, bordering on mildly funny, but I was sure I was alone in that opinion. Tim had a look of confusion on his face.

Justin went on with his act. "My neighbor across the street is an oncologist," he proclaimed. "She studies people who sit by the phone at night and on weekends waiting for their employer to call." I chuckled. Tim smiled. "Down at my local pawn and jewelry shop there is a guy who repairs time pieces that hang on walls. He's a clock-tologist. Speaking of -ologists, what do you call a doctor who specializes in treating people's faces after they've had really bad acne? A pock-tologist."

More people were getting up and leaving, but I was becoming more interested, even fascinated, with Justin's humor. The bartender yelled at Justin, "Tell them what's happening in August!" Justin nodded. "Oh, yes! Hey, everyone, you won't want to miss the comedy extravaganza next month, on August 15, right here at All This Alcohol Will Become Urine In Two Hours! A whole night of top-of-the-line comedians to thrill and kill! A pants-peeing, side-splitting good time will be had by all!"

I spoke up, feeling sheepish. "Carry on with your act, please. What else do you have?"

Justin turned his glance toward me and spoke without averting his gaze. "I was driving through the desert on I-50 in Nevada. I saw a sign that read, 'Report Shooting From Highway.' So I moved onto the shoulder and stopped. I got out my rifle and started blasting rocks and tin cans. Then I got my cell phone and called the number on the sign. 'Hello, I just want to be a good citizen and report that I'm shooting from the highway.'"

I couldn't hold it in any longer and let out an awkwardly long belly laugh. Justin tried not to smile at the pleasure of having at least one person who was getting his humor. A woman yelled out, "Are you done yet?" Justin looked over at the bartender, who yelled out, "One more!" The woman exhaled. "Thank God." Justin nodded in the bartender's direction, "She thanks God and I thank *you*, good sir."

I looked up at Justin and smiled again. He caught my gaze and said, "All right, I'll go now. But first, here's my last joke." He paused for a good five seconds to let anticipation build, then the complaining woman yelled, "Get on with it, I got a date with the restroom!" Justin ignored her and began. "A fly was ordering in a special sushi restaurant just for flies. The fly said to the waitress, 'I'll have the Horse Manure Roll, but I'm allergic to fake manure. What is this manure roll made from?' The waitress answered, 'We only use real manure here; no imitation crap is ever used.'"

I fell against Tim's shoulder, laughing uncontrollably. Tim looked at me as if I were the biggest weirdo *ever* and pushed me upright into my seat. I watched Justin turn and walk off. Tim said, "You're really enamored with him, aren't you?"

"Well, I'm not *enameled* with him, but I'd like to be!" I stood up and started walking in Justin's direction. Tim stood and grabbed my arm. "Where are you going?"

"To intro myself to Justin, where did you think?"

"Oh, okay. Shall I wait for you, or do you think you'll be busy the rest of the night?"

"Oh, don't be jealous, dear brother. I'll be back soon enough."

In truth, I wasn't back soon. I was busy the rest of the night getting to know Justin Jason-Jeremy. After I introduced myself to Justin, we talked easily for ten minutes. It was mutually apparent that we wanted to converse longer, and he asked me to meet him at Dimby's Barrel, a twenty-four-hour coffee house. I suddenly remembered I had told Tim I'd be back soon enough, but now I couldn't guarantee it. I told Justin I didn't have a ride and asked if I could go with him. I dashed back to where Tim was waiting and gave him my car key. "Sorry, Tim, I'm going to pick Justin's brain. Don't wait up." I share an apartment with my brother and didn't want him to worry about me.

Dimby's Barrel was jelly-packed, filled with late-night regulars from the bar who used the restaurant's food to soak up the copious amounts of alcohol in their tummies. Justin and I found two available stools at the counter, sat, and began to chat.

"I'm excited about the upcoming comedy extravaganza," I said.

Justin nodded enthusiastically. "Me too!" I told him that I loved his set because it wasn't obviously funny or cliché. He mock-frowned, "Okay, um, is that a good thing?"

"Oh, yes, for sure! I mean, it wasn't typical, predictable humor, right?"

He smiled. "Yeah, right. You got it!"

I asked him some common first-meeting questions. How did he get started in comedy? How often does he perform? What was the name of his first pet? Does he like it when a partner touches his periwinkle during lovemaking? He smiled politely.

I timidly shared a few select jokes of mine to get his reaction. "Hey, Justin, my friend Mark is one of the world's leading specialists at helping people get items off their floors and up onto accessible platforms in order to organize their homes. He's a shelf-help guru." He tilted his head and smiled. "Funny."

"When I read digital books before bed, I use a special kind of light fixture to see them: a Kindle-abra." Justin tilted his head again and rolled his eyes upward.

"Okay, very cute. Clever. I get it. It's very funny on one level and annoying on another level."

I scrunched my forehead skin. "What exactly do you mean?"

"Well, I mean that it's a comedy style that was popular long ago, but in some circles, it's a lost art form that's making a comeback."

I was relieved that he was giving constructive feedback. I hoped he wasn't just being nice so that he could get a free ticket to the inside of my pantaloons. I said, "Okay, give me one of yours."

He rocked his head side to side and rolled his eyes. "All right, here's one. I was registering on a website. Every time I entered a password that I thought was clever and easy for me to remember, a box would pop up with the word *Weak*. Every time I tried to make the password unusual and hard for a scammer to figure out, the box would pop up: *Weak*. On the fifth try, the box popped up and read *Weak but acceptable*. On my next try I typed in *Weak but acceptable* and the box popped up with *Strong!*"

I loved his humor. It was weird and unique. I wondered if we might blend our two humor types.

Justin said, "Okay, now give me one more."

I didn't know my jokes well enough to choose which would be best or better, so I just blurted out the next one that I could remember. "One of my employees has very bad credit and has to have his wages garnished. Every week when I hand him his paycheck, I am required by law to put orange slices and parsley on it."

He didn't react at first, but I could tell he was contemplating. "Kirsten. You are intrinsically funny. You need to keep doing this. Keep writing, and if you want to perform your material, you need to get out there and get some experience."

It seemed as though we had been at the restaurant for just a few minutes, but when I looked at my phone to check the time, I saw that we had been sitting at the counter for over two hours. We were both chuckling when a waitress approached to tell us the restaurant was closing in ten minutes. As we walked out to his car, Justin said, "Hey, the comedy extravaganza is happening soon. I'm going to sign up. You should too!"

I was flattered and terrified. "Oh, gosh, do you think I should?"

"Kirsten, I'm not blowing pollen up your petticoat

when I say that you are naturally funny. Yes, you should sign up and make your debut at the extravaganza!"

"All right then, I will! But I have to ask you, Justin, when do events *become* extravaganzas?"

He playfully said, "I'm not sure, Kirsten. When *do* events become extravaganzas?"

"When there are more vaganzas than you need!" He rolled his eyes. "*Extra* vaganzas. Get it?"

"Oh my goodness, Kirsten. Yes, I get it. You see? You are deeply funny."

* * *

The night of the comedy extra-vaganza finally arrived. I sat with dozens of moths in my tummy, waiting for the show to start. I had waffled, pancaked, and French-toasted back and forth, trying to decide whether to sign up. Ultimately, I needed to know how the general public would react to my style of humor. Thankfully my sweet, mellow, sometimes slightly clingy, mildly protective sibling Tim was in attendance to support me.

Oh, no! Here's the stage manager telling me I'm on now! Yikes! Wish me luck!

"Hello, all you lovely people. My name is Kirsten Kristen-Kiersten, and I'll be your stewardess for tonight. A friend recently asked me if I knew of a good massage therapist who doesn't cost an arm and a leg. I told her yes, I know one, but she only does arms and legs." A smattering of chuckles! Good start. "My cousin's dog, Rover, had to have an artificial foot surgically attached to one of his legs. Now he has a faux paw."

A guy called out, "When does the comedy portion of your show start?" Oh, great, my first heckler. I said to him, "Don't make me come over there and open this can of gentle-pat-on-the-butt!" That got bigger laughs than my jokes. Okay, duly noted.

"Last month I was driving through Sedona, Arizona, to attend a yoga and wheat-free bread-making retreat. I saw a bumper sticker on a car that read, 'Non-Judgment Day Is Near!'"

Some polite chuckling. Maybe I'm being too deep for this crowd?

"Hey, guys, on my driver license it reads that I'm a Wurlitzer and Kleenex donor. Are any of you Wurlitzer and Kleenex donors?"

Five long, slow seconds of silence. The faces I could see from the stage wore blank expressions. Then the same heckler yelled out, "What the flock are you talking about?"

I shot back, "I was hoping I wouldn't have to explain my jokes. Does anyone get it?"

A timid woman's voice came from over in the far stage-right corner. "Organ and tissue donors rule!" Oh, my goodness! She got it! (If you didn't get this joke either, Wurlitzer is a brand of music *organ* and, of course, Kleenex is *tissue*. Funny? Apparently only one lovely woman in the room thought so.)

"Moving right along. I really liked science projects as a kid. Did any of you like science class in school? I was especially drawn to wires and motors and switches. I decided that when I grew up I'd become an elocutionist."

Okay! Some definite guffaws. Maybe I should drop the oblique jokes and stay with simpler puns.

I tried one more. "My friend the lung doctor sidelined as an actor. She performed in a respiratory theater." That got a few chuckles. Okay, okay, not bad.

"Hey all, I've had a wonderful time. I will leave you with this. Standing in line at the airport, I overheard someone speaking into their phone, dictating some kind of message. This person said, 'Wine, doughnuts, beer, horse racing, bacon, whiskey, cigarettes, and adult movies.' They were *vice* texting." The timid woman in the back corner burst out laughing! A few others made sounds that I'll interpret to mean they thought it was amusing.

"Thank you all very much! Have a groovy night and life!"

I walked offstage and slinked up the side aisle to take a seat in the back, hoping no one would feel compelled to tell me that I'm a lousy comic. I wanted to catch Justin Jason-Jeremy's set. I sat through three more local comedians, all of whom ranged from meh to crap in my opinion. (I was trying not to be envious.)

Then Justin stepped onstage to close the Locals Only portion of the extravaganza. He put on a polished air of confidence. "Hello, I'm Justin Jason-Jeremy. I'm a full-time bread maker, and I also work nights and weekends as a self-employed private investigator." He paused to see if anyone responded. It was a provocative statement. Very smart. It sure got me wondering what he might say next. In four seconds, I started to silently snicker at the absurdity of a "bread maker/private eye."

"I hired one of my fellow bakery employees to assist me in figuring out a difficult case. I needed to know that I could trust my new assistant with sensitive information and told him sternly, 'At first, until I get to know you better, I'll be sharing the facts about a case on a knead-the-dough basis.'" Three seconds ticked by, then Justin got a decent amount of groans and giggles. I saw that comedy is as much about the delivery as the material.

Justin asked, "You know what I've been wondering about?" A woman shouted, "I've been wondering what you look like naked." That was weird and funny. Most of the audience chortled. Justin grinned widely, and I could tell he lost his place for a few seconds. "Thank you, ma'am. I'm sure that soon we'll all have X-ray apps on our phones and you won't have to wonder anymore." *Oh good, he recovered*, I thought.

"The fact is, I've been wondering about the last bastion. What about the *first* bastion? Why is it always the *last* one? Poor bastion. When choosing sides for basketball at school, always last." This time he hit many funny bones and got a decent laugh across the whole crowd. I liked that Justin didn't leave too much time for the audience to lose their connection with him.

Sometimes he'd follow a joke with an out-of-left-field statement, like this: "I now interrupt my routine to ask you something of great importance. Am I the first person to notice that the first six notes of the song 'Crystal Ship' by the Doors are the same first six notes of 'It Was a Very Good Year (When I Was Seventeen)' made famous by Frank Sinatra?" I sang the lines in my head. Weird. He's right. Cool!

He had the audience sing both first lines with him to prove his point. "'Before you slip into...' Now let's do the other song. 'When I was seventeen...'" The audience loved it! He was now officially on a roll. I was digging Justin more and more.

"I've been learning Spanish in my spare time. I use an online language program that teaches useful phrases like, *Mi tortuga usa un tutú rosa, juega al Scrabble con nuestro oso hormiguero, y tiene las axilas peludas.* (My turtle wears a pink tutu, plays Scrabble with our anteater, and has hairy armpits.) I winced. Justin didn't get much reaction from that one. I could tell he knew it and was scrambling to get the audience back with him. He picked up the speed of his delivery.

"Hey, tell me, where are all the Buddhist science reading rooms?

"I was watching TV this morning. The announcer said, 'Coming up tonight after the six o'clock news, we will air a special report, When Good Things Happen To Bad People.'

"Have you ever noticed that sweatpants on a man make his butt appear smaller and sweatpants on a woman makes her butt look bigger?

"I was just deleting emails in my junk folder. The subject line of one read Wild Orgy Invitation. I thought, *are there different kinds of orgies? Or is just the invitation wild?*

"After preparing tofu for cooking, be sure to thoroughly wash all surfaces and utensils with hot water and soap to prevent the spread of bacteria, said no one, *ever*.

"When I think of all the amazing inventions over the last 120 years—cars, airplanes, radios, TVs, air conditioning, computers—the most impressive one is the *Unfollow* button on Facebook." Justin was doing okay there for a while, but that one missed the mark. He wisely decided to end his set.

"Hey, it's been a blast up here. I want to thank the owners of All This Alcohol Will Become Urine In Two Hours and the manager of The Dreaded Plateau for having me. Thank you to all the amazing local comedians who performed earlier. Stick around the rest of the night for more comedy."

People had been dawdling out for the last five minutes of his set. I wanted Justin to get an encore, so I started chanting, "One more! One more! One more!" Several people joined in, and the bartender raised his right index finger, giving Justin the universal signal of "okay, one more."

Justin smiled and said with a burst of energy, "All right! Hey, give me a 'hell yeah' if you agree that seamless rain gutters *rock*!" The room continued to empty out as one restrained voice said, "Heck yes." It was the timid-voiced woman who had spoken up during my set. I was so embarrassed for Justin that I chickened out and didn't say anything. The bartender yelled across the room, "That was your last one!" Justin sheepishly said, "Yes, that *was* my last one."

* * *

The audience had filled the room again, and the next extravaganza act had been onstage for a while.

"No, you idiot! It's because you're nineteen!"

The eruption of laughter was so loud it rivaled the noise at the start of the Indianapolis 500. The rowdy crowd inside The Dreaded Plateau comedy room fell about the place at hearing Tawdry Boorish the Vulgarian deliver his first joke. An up-and-coming comic, he had told this joke more than thirty-seven times at The Dreaded Plateau over the last twelve months, and it was still hilarious to most of the patrons.

Tawdry Boorish the Vulgarian is, obviously, a vulgar comic. In fact, his jokes are so bad that I can't repeat them here. He isn't the dirtiest comedian I've ever heard, but his specialty is mild raunch. If his jokes could be poured over a salad, you'd call them Mild Raunch Dressing. Sorry, I can't help it. If I were in an addicts' support group, I'd introduce myself by saying, "My name is Kirsten, and I was born to create puns." Well, actually, I don't *create* them, they *find* me. They travel *through* me from the nether regions of planet Puntovia.

Justin tilted his head toward the stage and looked at me. "Are you paying attention to the way the crowd responds to him?"

"Oh, yes, Justy, I most certainly am!" I answered.

Tawdry Boorish the Vulgarian has a contract with every establishment at which he performs, with a requirement that anytime he is written about or verbally addressed, his entire name must be used. Not Tawd or Tawdry or Tawdry Boorish, but Tawdry Boorish the Vulgarian.

"How y'all doin' tonight, ya sums-a-bee-atches?!"

Tawdry Boorish the Vulgarian yelled into the mic. "I don't know about you morons, but when I see crowds like this, or pictures of huge crowds at concerts or sporting events, I contemplate the fact that all those people took a dump today! Wow! Can you imagine? Sixty thousand people all crappin' at once, and all that crap floatin' down the sewer pipe of life! Hey, that's a nice metaphor, ain't it? *Metaphor* is a funny word, ain't it? It looks and sounds like something you'd put on an open wound. 'Hey, honey, I got a huge ugly rash on my balls. Can ya bring me that bottle of Metaphor?' Speakin' of dumps, the older I get, the more I enjoy takin' a dump. I enjoy it as much as I enjoy eatin'. And speakin' of eatin', the other night I was at a restaurant full of people chompin' and chewin'. It was disgusting! I looked around and thought, *why do we have to* buy *food?* It should be rented, not purchased. The chefs work really hard to make all these nice gourmet meals that are gonna end up in the toilet tomorrow!" He paused to let the laughter die down a bit before he got back into his routine.

"I'm a lonely, single dork, right? Everyone knows it. Yesterday I was opening a new account on a website, and I had to provide answers to the security questions. The first one was: In which city did you meet your right hand?"

I poked Justin on the shoulder and yelled in his ear, "Let's go. I've had enough of Tawdry Boorish the Vulgarian!"

He nodded in agreement. We made our way out through the boozy, compacted crowd, not caring about the many butt and boob grazes that we couldn't avoid (and that we mutually enjoyed.) As we bobbed and weaved our way out, Tawdry Boorish the Vulgarian called out, "Hey, you two morons! There ain't nothin' more important than what's going on right here!" I shouted to Justin, "Don't turn around! Don't answer him!" We pushed on through to the exit door as Tawdry Boorish the Vulgarian told the crowd, "Those two halfwits must be in a hurry to get to the half-off sale on brains across the street at Body Parts R Us." Outside on the sidewalk, we heard the crowd proclaiming its approval of Tawdry Boorish the Vulgarian's disparagement of us.

Justin said, "First, I love that you, as the narrator of this story, used *disparagement* in a sentence. Second, his popularity still baffles me. Notwithstanding, I do see that he appeals to a particularly dimwitted type of audience, and that in itself is one way to build a career."

I said, "First, Justy, I admire you for using *notwithstanding* in a sentence. Second, I liberally concur with your perceptive, poignant pontification. I'm certain beyond a shadow of a turd that I don't want to be a vulgar comedian."

"Okay, but it could ultimately lead to a lot of money. Don't give up just yet. Have you tried writing any vulgar jokes?"

"Yes, I have a few," I replied.

Justin nodded, "Okay, give me one. Pretend I'm a judge on that talent show, America's Got Vulgarity."

I searched my half-off brain for the best of my crude jokes. "Okay, I got it. Are you ready?"

"Yes, I'm ready. Hit me with your best endeavor." (I like that he used *endeavor* in a sentence.)

"Yesterday I was fondling myself on my way to Chicago, and boy is my arm tired."

Justin shook his head. "Yeah. No. Please don't."

"Oh, believe me, I won't," I said. "I don't want to build a career on an audience of dimwits. What if, at some point in the future, they started socializing with puritanical people, reading self-help books and evolving? I'd lose my devotees!"

As we stood outside, we heard the end of Tawdry Boorish the Vulgarian's set. "Thank you, clowns, you're so nice! I've had a great time, I hope you did too. Here's one more. Do you want one more?" The crowd demanded another. He rambled along, describing a crass and uncouth scenario, then dumped the punchline. A huge applause and raucous laughter as Tawdry Boorish the Vulgarian dropped the mic.

"It's the *way* he says it," I said. "It's not a great joke, but he *makes* it great!"

"I get your point," Justin admitted. "But I still say his humor is stupid. He relies on infantile crudeness for laughs."

"Yeah? So what?" I said. "Infantile crudeness is currently king in this comedy climate. He's starting to get noticed around town. Next thing you know, he'll get that coveted first appearance on the Even Later with Johnny Autodaughter Show!"

Justin replied, "First of all, I'm impressed that you used *coveted* in a sentence. Second of all, Johnny Autodaughter will make him tone down his raunch on TV, but Tawdry Boorish the Vulgarian needs to be on full raunch to be funny!"

"I'm just bummed out that no one seems to care about my style of clean comedy!" I pouted.

"Hey, let's relocate to Burger Dump on La Brea for a while. I think we can skip the next one or two comics."

* * *

We walked to my car, got in, and cruised from The Dreaded Plateau to Burger Dump in my pile-of-excrement 1986 Oldsmobile Calais Supreme with Justin in the passenger seat and Tim in the back. Tim couldn't stop complimenting me. "Hey, sis! I never knew you could be so funny! I mean it. You have something special going on!" I thanked him but sat quietly, contemplating vulgar comics as I let my inferiority complex and envy of Tawdry Boorish the Vulgarian percolate.

Justin suddenly punctured the silence. "You have a crush on him, don't you?"

I wrinkled my forehead and, without turning my gaze from the road, said, "That's just stupid. Why would you say that?"

Tim said, "Because every time we see him perform, you rave about him, defend his raunchy style, and start talking about giving up on your clean comedy."

"So that means I have a crush on him? Sheesh, guys, are you both eight years old?" I started to get that telltale pre-blubber quiver in my lower lip and chin.

Tim softened. "Oh, honey, I'm sorry. We didn't mean to nudge that nerve."

"I might as well tell you both." I looked over at Justin, then in the rearview mirror to catch Tim's eye. "I'm not so sure I want to try making it as a clean comic. It seems like an uphill battle, banging my head against the repugnant trend."

Justin blurted out, "We should start a band!" I tilted my head, dog-like. "What? Why?"

"So we can call ourselves Repugnant Trend! No, wait. *The* Repugnant Trend. Let's bring back that long-forgotten time when bands had a *The* before their name." I ignored his attempt to cheer me up.

I drove around behind Burger Dump to my secret parking spot between the huge, filthy, overflowing dumpster and the rear entrance of Oh Phuque Mie Tax Preparation. We strolled listlessly around to the front door.

"Justin, do you think I was born fifty years too late?" Justin and Tim looked at each other, then at me, but didn't say anything. "I say that because it seems that my sense of humor is exactly what Americans loved in the 1940s and '50s. It's simple, innocent, and pun-based. We all know that the most popular current comedians are profane and vulgar. But I've been saddled with this, this... *thing*. Whether it's a gift or a curse, I don't know."

We entered the eatery. I slumped into a booth while Tim and Justin slid in opposite me. Justin said, "Well, there is that old saying, 'Don't punch a saddled cursehorse in the mouth.' By the way, just so we're on the same leaflet, what exactly *is* this gift or curse of which you speak?"

"It's the damn constant incoming silly puns and jokes! I can't turn them off! They enter my brain all night and day!"

"Oh, Kirsten, do you know how many comedians would give their left ovary to have this gift-slash-curse of yours?"

"You mean comediennes, don't you?" I asked. "And speaking of that, when did people stop calling female comedians *comediennes* and start calling them the unisex *comedian*?"

"Right. Who was president when that transpired?" Tim asked.

"What was the name of the horse that won the Kentucky Derby that year?" I said.

Justin threw in, "Surely there was a huge socio-political event, such as a Hollywood celebrity caught fondling himself inside a crypto coin laundry while unabashedly leering at *Modern Laundromat* magazine to time stamp the sudden stoppage of the use of *comedienne*?"

"You see?!" I blurted. "We're a good fit and a good team, Justin!"

He mumbled, "Well, yeah, okay. Maybe. But you didn't compliment me for using *unabashedly* in a sentence." We rolled our eyes at each other.

I pointed to Tim. "Do keep in mind, dearest Justin and Tim, that I don't have unlimited time to make this comedy thing happen. Tim, you know our parents have urged—no, *demanded*—that I go into the comedy field since I was ten years old. After high school graduation, they said they would support me if I gave comedy a huge, concerted effort. If, after six years of trying, comedy just didn't work out, they would cut off their funding but allow me to go for my first love of mechanical engineering. I'm currently in year four of that six-year plan. Now I have amassed so many jokes that I feel I can't just stop, just give it all up. What else can I do with all this material?"

Justin said, "First, I like that you used *amassed* in a sentence. Second, you could put a book of all your jokes that nobody needs out into the world, and nobody will ever know about it or read it because you're unknown and it will be buried deep inside the digital wasteland."

"Oh, Justin, what a wonderful comfort and friend you are," I said with a heaping tablespoonful of irony.

Tim said, "Kirsten, dear, you're on year four of a six-year plan, right?" I nodded. "That means we have two years for you to achieve some sort of success!"

Justin added, "Two whole years!" Tim smiled and nodded ardently.

I revealed, "Even though I'm working at it and trying to get somewhere in comedy, I hate the feeling of being a wannabe. Most of the time, I feel like a damn hobbyist, as if I'm taking up space that belongs to the comics who are desperately trying to make a living at it. And I hate the feeling of being envious when I hear about another local comic having success! I want to be supportive, but it's such a self-centered pursuit and hard scramble to the top that I often get whipped into an envious lather when I hear of anyone in any field of entertainment who achieves success."

Justin squinted his eyes and got serious for a moment, "You have to go for it! Would you rather be a has-been or a wannabe?"

I said, "That's deep, Justy. Do you mind if I occasionally just call you *Justy* or *Just* or *Justfellow?*"

"I don't mind. Just don't call me J-man, J-dude, or Justina."

Tim said, "Ooh. I like Justina!"

Without turning, Justin pointed his finger toward Tim. "Don't."

I said, "Before I answer whether I would rather be a has-been or a wannabe, I have to tell you that I was at Barnes and Noble last week and there was an old actor having a book signing. Instead of thinking *good for him*, I'm embarrassed to say that I got so envious that I had to leave! I kept having those ugly thoughts of *Why him? Why not me? When is it going to be my turn?* I don't want to be a wannabe anymore!"

As I pondered my situation and let my rolling eyeballs explore the inside of the restaurant, I said, "Burger Dump is actually a nice place, isn't it?"

"Yes. You're quite correct." Justin agreed.

I said, "It's the name that makes it. I think the owners are fans of irony."

"Isn't Irony a band?" asked Justin. I let on a wee little smile (like someone from Ireland might do), and sent him a furtive glance to acknowledge his joke. "I think my cousin attended their big show when they opened for Satire."

"OMG, Justin! That's really good! You've got the disease, too! We should be writing partners!" He backed away. "Oh, no, I can't keep up with you."

"Okay" I said, "but may I use that joke?"

He smiled, "Only if you let me be the bus driver on your forty-city tour of Punistan."

On the drive back to the comedy extravaganza, I asked Justin if he would play a little word game with me to see if we would make good partners. He said, "Okay, I'm *game*. Go ahead."

"All right, here we go. Answer each question with a query of your own," I said. "Do you turn drinking glasses and coffee cups upside down in the cupboard, as if insects are going to climb into them?"

"Are you one of those types who can't have different foods touching each other on your plate?"

"Do you say *easy-over* eggs instead of *over-easy*?"

"Do you say *woyer* instead of *warrior*?"

"Do you say *goff* instead of *golf*?"

"Do you screw on the peanut butter jar lid crooked and think it's okay to leave it like that?"

"Ooh, good one, Justin. When you drive someone else's car, do you change the seat position, heater setting, and radio station but don't put them back where they were?"

"When you spend the night in a hotel, do you tighten up the sheets and blanket, smoothing and tucking everything in perfectly in the morning, knowing it's going to be harder for the maids to pull it all apart, instead of just leaving the bed unmade?"

I knew we'd be good together, I thought. I went on. "As Douglas Fergus wrote in his wonderful book *Small Portions Café*, do you leave kitchen sponges soaking wet in the bottom of the sink?"

"Do you like sickeningly overripe, almost-black bananas?" he said.

"Are you one of those weirdos who doesn't like mustard, raisins, and chopped olives in your tuna salad?"

"Are you one of those dipsticks who likes runny egg yolks?"

"Are you one of those morons who gets nauseated if your egg yolks are the slightest bit runny?" I said.

"Are you one of those dorkmeisters who orders your eggs *sunny up* instead of *sunny-side up*?"

"Basically, I hope you're not one of those people who starts every sentence with *basically*."

Justin said, "Do you leave half a mouthful of milk in the bottle so that you won't be the one who finished off the milk?"

I beamed at him. "I think we'll get along supremely, smashingly well!" We paid our bill and headed back to The Dreaded Plateau and the extravaganza.

* * *

As we stepped into the club, we heard the comedy going down. The performer who was about to come on was Sadie Socko. Pretty, fifty-five-ish, five foot five-ish, shoulder-length blonde hair, witty and quick, like a blonde Julia Louis-Dreyfus. Sadie had performed all over North America for fifteen years and had appeared hundreds of times on television. She was so loved and adored for her clever jokes that her fans had memorized all her routines, so much so that Sadie had transitioned to telling only the punchlines to her famous jokes. Over the years, she had faded from the big time but still retained a small, rabid fan base who attended all her performances.

Sadie walked out onstage to a welcoming applause. She stood at the mic for more than fifteen seconds, letting the tension build. The crowd began to chatter about which punchline she'd open with. "I saw her in Boise four years ago," a man said loudly to his neighbor. "She killed with, 'I was talking to the pig.'" Sadie bellowed, "I heard that! I'm *not* going to tell that one!" The crowd giggled with delight. After another long pause, she calmly said, "For a nickel I will." The audience cackled with glee.

She proceeded to throw out punchline after punchline. "I can't tell her the truth!" "Now, walk slowly toward me." "Because it only rains on Tuesdays!" She clearly enchanted her people. She ended her set with the age-old, "No, Dad! Pie are *round*! *Cornbread* are square!" As she left the stage, the audience began chanting, "Sa-*die*! Sa-*die*! Sa-*die*!" Sadie disappeared behind the curtain for several seconds, then came bounding back up to the mic. She pointed at the man who had seen her in Boise four years ago and said, "This is for you, buddy!" She paused while scanning the audience, left to right, up and back, then looked directly at the man. "I was talking to the pig." The place roared its approval.

Next up was a guy who had been traveling the country doing cover jokes. I know. Weird, right? I thought only rock bands did covers of other people's material. But he was surprisingly good. His gift was his unique rendering of each joke or bit. Like most cover musicians, he probably didn't have the gift of creating original material, but he didn't let that stop him from being an entertainer. He began by telling that old Gallagher bit, "Why do hot dog *buns* come eight to a pack but *hot dogs* come ten to a pack?" And, "Why are rental houses called apart-ments when they're built so close together?"

Next, he told a Seinfeld bit. "On airplanes, they show you how to use the seatbelt in case you haven't been in a car since 1965. 'Oh, you lift *up* on the buckle! Oh! I was trying to break the metal apart. I thought that was how it worked.'"

He closed his set with a Rodney Dangerfield gem. "My psychiatrist told me I'm going crazy. I told him, 'If you don't mind, I'd like a second opinion.' He said, 'All right. You're ugly, too!'"

My envy kicked in while watching him perform. His routine was effortless. He looked like he was simply talking to a friend. The audience loved him! I yelled in Justin's ear, "My low self-esteem is kicking in because he's onstage, where I want to be, but here I am in the audience, a pitiful wannabe."

Justin shouted back, "You're not a wannabe. Wannabes are wishers, not workers, and that's not the way, for what comes too easily is thrown away!"

I shouted, "I can hardly hear you! Let's go outside!" We pushed our way out again to the comfort of the sidewalk.

Justin tried to lift my spirits by telling me that the audience didn't care (maybe weren't even aware) that the cover comedian was delivering a joke that he didn't write. He said, "I saw a cover band play "Taking Care of Business" last Friday night at the Spotless Pig Bar and

Grill over on La Cienega. People went bonkers! Within fifteen seconds they were shouting the lyrics, guzzling beer, stomping their feet, jumping up on chairs and tables, and pumping their fists. Imagine if a person in the audience approached the stage, stopped the band from playing, turned to the crowd, and yelled, 'Hey, gang! This band didn't write this song! It was originally written and recorded by the members of Bachman-Turner Overdrive! The band here wishes they had written it, but they're just lowly cover musicians! They aren't that creative!' Do you think everyone would suddenly be disappointed and walk out? Of course not. The performance is what matters."

"I hear you, Justy," I said. "Thank you for the moxie talk. I'm fighting the wannabe feeling by telling myself that my gift to the world is my original material, and because I'm not fully evolved, it makes me feel superior to this cover comedian. Then I feel bad for thinking that I'm a better human than him. Maybe he's a really nice, humble, grateful person. Here I am trashing him when I don't even know him at all! Gall-dang it!"

Justin smiled "You said 'gall-dang it.'"

I shrugged my shoulders and started to pout. "Maybe I'm not meant to be a performer."

"Not so fast, fanny frown," Justin said enthusiastically. "We have two more years to make some kind of mark in the comedy world! Two more years!"

We made our way back inside just in time to hear the emcee give a bouncy introduction to a nostalgia-comedy team. "Please extend a tepid welcome to Phyllis Rivers and Milton Hope." The duo opened their set with a version of what is likely the first joke ever written.

"Hey, Phyllis, I just flew in from Poughkeepsie."

"Oh, really, Milton? How do you feel?"

"Well, gosh, Phyllis. My arms are really tired!"

I turned to Tim. "I can't believe they actually told that one."

He said, "They're a classic nostalgia act, right?" I nodded in agreement. "If they didn't tell that one, people would be asking for a refund."

Phyllis and Milton carried on with their act to varying degrees of groans and guffaws, giving the people what they wanted to hear. They closed with this gem: "Hey, Phyllis, did you hear that Gene Gene made a machine?"

"Oh, really, Milton? What did he do with it?"

"He gave it to Jo Jo."

"Gosh, Milton, what did Jo Jo do with it?"

"You won't believe it, Phyllis, but he made it go."

"That's interesting, Milton, because rumor has it that Art Art was involved."

"You're correct, Phyllis. He cut a fart and blew it all apart!"

The adolescent part of everyone's brain smiled and applauded robustly.

Next up was a tribute act. This type of comic proudly announces that they are performing the material of a particular famous comedian. The fans demand that the act be as close as possible to an exact impersonation of the original. The comic was billed as George and the Carlins – A Tribute to George Carlin. He rattled off several of

Carlin classic bits about television, religion, farts, politics, and stuff with such hilarious precision that he made us all believe George didn't die in 2008, he just went into hiding for a few years and resurfaced as a tribute comic of himself.

Following the Carlin tribute, we saw Fairbruce McDoeglass, a comedian with more than eight followers on social media. He was carrying on the well-worn tradition of comics who told the-difference-between-men-and-women jokes. He's known for his deadpan style and not talking between jokes.

"Why do women fold towels lengthwise in thirds? They're experts at it from birth. They hold one end between their chin and chest, letting the towel hang down. They magically fold it lengthwise into perfect thirds, then perfectly fold it all the way down. I can't do it. It's physically impossible for me. I fold towels in half and then half again. Easy. Women will even fold a damp dish towel lengthwise in thirds then hang it over the handle on the oven. How is it supposed to dry when it's *folded?* Men hang damp dish towels over the entire width of the oven handle without folding because we know that's the only way they will dry. Sure, it's not as pretty as a towel folded in thirds, but we know that's the fastest way for a towel to dry, right?

"For my birthday, my wife said she'd give me a twenty-four-hour period to put anything I want on any horizontal surface in the house. Isn't she nice? I went berserk and ran through the house, emptying my pockets, sprinkling all the surfaces with keys, pens, pocket screwdrivers, coins, blown automotive fuses, ketchup packets, blue and yellow electrical wire nuts, marbles, sheet-metal screws, an empty tube of strawberry-flavored ChapStick, a sewing thimble, and an old business card from a carpet sales company that closed four years ago. I had written 'Bronco '71 $28K Dave 906-8321' on the back.

"I came home from work the next day, and *all* my stuff was gone! All horizontal surfaces had been vacated. There was now a small wicker basket on the half-wall between the entry and kitchen. I peered down into the basket and, yep, all my stuff was neatly arranged inside. As my wife walked toward me from the living room, she said with a smile, 'See? Isn't this great? All your things are nice and neat in one place.' I said, 'Do I have to keep everything neat inside the basket? Or can I just dump stuff in there?'

"She frowned. 'Why would you *dump* stuff in there? The purpose is to keep everything neat and tidy.' 'Um,' I said with trepidation. 'I truly love that you've put a lot of thought into this and that you've obtained a nice basket for this purpose, but I don't want to carefully, neatly put things in there. I want a place to just dump things.'

"She took a deep breath, exhaled noisily, and stood there quietly long enough for me to silently sing 'Bohemian Rhapsody' in its entirety before she spoke again. She squinted her eyes and said in a monotone, 'Where do you think you're going to get twenty-eight thousand dollars to buy Dave's Bronco?'

"'Honey,' I said, 'I love this basket idea!'"

All right, he was good. I appreciated his humor.

I turned to Justin and said, "Hey, Justy, we can't miss the closing act. She's the newest, hottest new comedian, and I've got to check her out. You should too. I've heard through the rumor factory that she's odd, witty, fickle, and beguiling."

Justin said, "I like Odd, Witty, Fickle and Beguiling. They represented me in my iguana custody case against my ex."

I chuckled. "And that's why I want you on my team, Justy!"

He smiled, "Let's take a break and meet back here at eight-oh-five."

We walked off in separate directions. He turned and yelled, "What's the name of this new comedian?!"

I yelled back, "Bileigh Aighlash!"

He shouted, "How do you spell that?"

I shouted back, "T-H-A-T!" He shook his head, turned, and marched away.

✱ ✱ ✱

Per our plan, Justin and I met back at the club and pushed our way through the audience to meet up with Tim. He had tried to hold spots for us, but it was already SRO, so we just stayed squeezed in with the crowd. The emcee appeared from behind the curtain, and the enthusiastic, anticipatory crowd burst into applause.

Bileigh Aighlash was signed with a prestigious management firm that was carefully controlling her publicity. Information about her was revealed drip by drip on social media in order to keep fans hungry for her. Her brilliant personal manager knew exactly what people wanted to know. So far, the only things he released to media outlets were her favorite food, waist size, and videos of her cleaning up her kitten's vomit.

"Hello, you lovely humans!" bellowed the emcee. "Here she is, the human bean that you have been pining, oaking, and maple-ing for, Bileigh Aighlash!"

Bileigh strolled up to the mic and got right into it. "Um, like, like, like, um, like, like, I'm all, like, um." The crowd chuckled loudly. "I'm all, like, like, um, like, like, um, like, like, like, like." Louder laughing and applause.

Justin looked over at me and yelled, "Am I in a dream?! WTF is going on?!"

I yelled in his ear, "You don't know? How have you avoided being bombarded with her deets on Feeba, Insta, Twit, Tik, and every remaining newspaper and stone tablet?"

He shook his head and shrugged his shoulders.

"I'll have to tell you outside after her set. It's too much information to tell you now!"

We turned back to the stage. Bileigh rattled off, "Um, um, um, like, like, like, like, like, like like, like, um, like, like, like." Now the crowd whooped and ululated.

Justin hollered, "What the heck is so gall-dang funny?!"

His demeanor got meaner. I turned and pulled his arm. "Let's go out front. I'll explain!" As we bounced like pinballs through the crowd on our way out of the club, people looked at us as if we were completely crazy for leaving during Bileigh's set. We pushed out the door and stopped on the sidewalk.

"All right, Justin. Here's everything I know about Bileigh. I got all this info from her Wikipedia page—and yes, *I donated $2.95 to keep them from bankruptcy, dammit!* You obviously know about the government program called SFSLYMK! (Stop Fricking Saying *Like*, You Moronic Kids!) that was designed to stop young people from overusing the word *like*, right?"

Justin nodded his head and recited the rules. "'All citizens aged twelve to eighteen must wear a government-applied and controlled shock collar that zaps them if they say the word *like* more than once per thirty-minute time period.'" I was impressed that he could recite the rule.

"That's right, Justy! Bileigh began writing jokes and performing locally when she was sixteen. She hated the shock collar so much that she fibbed and told her grandpa that she lost the key to her bike lock and needed to borrow his bolt cutters. She then cut off her shock collar and threw it into the nearby Cement Galoshes river. This, of course, caused the collar tracking system computer to go on high alert at SFSLYMK! headquarters. She's had to lie low, stay under the radar, and belly crawl under the barbed wire of life ever since, for fear of being caught by the SFSLYMK! police. As a result, she's become a hero to millions. She so hated the government trying to stamp out young people's use of the word that she now says only *like* and a few other wasteful non-words such as *I'm like*, *I'm all*, *uh*, and *um*."

Justin was perplexed. "How do people know what she's actually saying? Is everyone else hearing what I'm hearing, just a whole bunch of *likes*?"

I went easy on him. "First, Justy, do you like that I used *perplexedly* in my narration?" He shot me a fantastic deadpan look that made me bust out a guffaw. "In truth, only the super-hip know what she's saying. Everyone else is just pretending to know."

"Either way," he said, "it's still just pretending to know, right?"

"Yes, I suppose so, my Justfellow."

He paused in contemplation and softened a bit. "I suppose that whatever she's doing is working," he said matter-of-factly. "Let's go back inside and catch the end of her set."

I opened the door to the club. It was so packed that we had to stand just inside the entrance. It was obvious that Bileigh was buoyed by the fantastic response to her routine. Her voice was stronger, louder, and more confident than it had been when we had stepped outside.

She delivered her closing joke. "Like, um, I'm all, like, like, like, like, like, like, um, like." The assemblage thundered its approval. I would compare it to a scaled-down version of the sound inside a football stadium when the first baseman kicks a strike into the touchdown basket over the home plate net.

Justin and I quickly slipped out the front door as the crowd's chatter rose to a feverish volume. "Wow," he exclaimed. "Bileigh has arrived!"

* * *

Two days after the comedy extravaganza, I was flopped out on the living room couch at the apartment I share with Tim. He and Justin were flopped somewhere else, maybe on the floor. It was summer, there was no air conditioning, and we were stripped to our underwear, passing a huge bottle of peppermint schnapps back and forth, getting buzzed beyond belief and watching MTV. (I will assume that you, smart reader, have already noted that Buzzed Beyond Belief would be a fantastic band name.)

I had put my cell phone in the waistband of the boy shorts I had borrowed from Tim because all my undies were in the dirty clothes hamper. (Well, he *is* my brother, right?) Just as an anonymous rapper on MTV was showing us his gold-plated master bath toilet, my phone vibrated. I pulled it from the elastic band and saw a number I didn't know. I almost didn't answer it, but in my buzzed condition I thought, *why the heck not?*

"Helloooohhh," I answered in a sing-songy way, then struggled to comprehend what the person was saying. Within seconds the fog lifted and I was crisp, clear-headed, and coherent. "Yes, sir. Three o'clock. Thursday the twenty-sixth. Got it! Thank you!" I completely sobered up after hearing that Aliyah wanted to see me! I quickly opened the Notes app on my phone and voice texted, "Yes sir three o'clock Thursday the twenty-sixth got it thank you."

Tim and Justin started yelling. "What?" "Who was that?" "Tell us!"

I said, "I hope that wasn't a prank. The guy said he's Aliyah's manager. Got my number from the bar. Aliyah was incognito at the extravaganza and saw my set! She loved it and wants me to come back for another audition!"

Tim jumped up and yelled, "Yes to the sidekick callback, baby!"

Justin smiled but wasn't so enthusiastic. He said, "I guess now it's time to admit that you've been right all along."

I asked, "What do you mean?"

"We *should* be a team. We write alike, we think alike. I have no problem riding on your coattails."

I jumped up. "Oh, Justy! At last you've swayed my way! And I have no problem pulling you along on my coattails!"

Tim chimed in. "Um . . . I can hear you. Am I being excluded from this party?"

"Oh, Timothy, of course not! But I thought you were focusing on your dance career."

"Well, lately I've been feeling that my true calling is co-writing jokes with you. Haven't you noticed my contributions? I mean, isn't critiquing your material kinda the same as co-writing?"

I said, "Oh, um, well, yeah, I guess."

Justin jumped in. "What she's saying is, *yes*, Tim! Of course! We want and need you on our team! Don't waste your time with dance classes. Let's build a comedy empire!"

"That's right, Timmy! It's time for you to pick a stream and paddle!"

He looked relieved and happy. "All right, musketeers!" he declared. "I hereby commit myself to this team because we are too legitimate to quitimate!"

* * *

I worked with Tim and Justin to make sure my—I mean *our*—jokes would knock Aliyah's knickers off. I retrieved my notebooks and a shoebox from the top shelf of my closet. The shoebox was full of paper scraps, napkins, and Post-It notes containing hundreds of silly puns and hastily scratched-out concepts that surely would become some of the funniest jokes ever told. Justin brought twelve thumb drives full of buffoonery, tomfoolery, and wisecracks. Even Tim had hastily scribbled out some ideas of his own.

We dropped all the material into the comedy colander. Out of the bottom, the golden dregs came trickling out. We sifted, arranged, and rearranged all the goods for my three-minute audition. My goal was to show Aliyah that we have a knack for creating cute, clean, clever, crazy comedy that would cultivate cackling and chuckles in clowns, cardinals, captains, clairvoyants, conductors, concierges and people with the funny name of Clapsaddle.

I practiced alone in our apartment while Tim was gone. I read the set aloud to the applause of the toaster, the refrigerator, the bookshelf, a Neil Diamond album, and a chair. I clocked my time at less than three minutes.

The next morning Justin and Tim came over to critique the set. They settled in, ready with notepads and pencils.

"I have a friend who is a practicing Mormon. He's in a motorcycle gang with fellow Mormons. They call themselves Heck's Angels." Justin and Tim chuckled. I went on.

"I have a friend who was dating an heiress to the Samsonite family fortune, but he had to break up with her because she had too much baggage." They chuckled again—barely.

"Amelia the English teacher specializes in punctuation. A colonoscopy revealed she had cancer and some of her intestines had to be removed. Now she has a semicolon. Speaking of English, have you ever noticed that the word *textile* has nothing to do with texting or tile?" Tim and Justin were getting a little restless.

"I found out yesterday there is a book about organizing dishes and dry goods in your kitchen cabinets in a very methodical way. It's written by L. Ron Cupboard. Still speaking English, it's an interesting language, isn't it? I love phrases like 'Slaughter is the best medicine.' And hey, what's with farm-raised fish? Did they have to do chores? Milk the cows? Drive a tractor? Feed the chickens?" I got a little giggle for that one.

"How many of us have been on the phone on hold, waiting *forever* for a customer service agent from a foreign country to help us with a technical problem? It's a big pain, right? When you want to speed up your wait time, take a big bite of food! The representative will immediately come on the line, but they won't wait for you to finish eating it and will hang up on you. And what about people in India who call for computer tech support? Are they connected to a person in Oklahoma?" A smile from Tim and a thumbs up from Justin.

"My neighbor's Aunt Griselda is a self-employed professional picture taker. On a whaling expedition, she brought her camera but forgot her spear, so she was a lance-free photographer." The smiles from Tim and Justin were all fine and good, but I wanted laughs. Smiles won't win me the audition.

"I was approached by an actor who played a motorcycle-riding 1950s greaser-type character in a popular TV show from the 1970s. He convinced me to invest money in his new company, which he promised would generate huge financial returns. I fell for it, gave him thousands, but ended up destitute and homeless. Turns out it was a Fonzie scheme." I got a real laugh on that one.

"A package delivery person needed me to sign his clipboard. He said, 'Give me your John Henry on the dotted line.' I said, 'Do you mean my John Hancock?' He replied, 'Who is John Hancock? No. I need your John Henry.' I said, 'Okay, let me get my railroad spike and sledgehammer and I'll sign that for you.'" I ended the set with a little bow.

Justin and Tim applauded heartily.

"Yes, Justy, what did you think?"

He looked over at Tim. "Um... don't hate me because you're beautiful, but I think we can do better." My face dropped, and I exhaled out of my nose, deflated.

"Crap! Gall and the Dang-Its! I know you're right!"

Justin said, "Hey, we all put that set together, so let's dig up some more gems and make it even better."

We sat on the living room floor all afternoon and into the night working on another version of the act. Around eight o'clock that evening, Tim walked down the street to get pizza. He came back with a pizza box in one hand and a gigantic bottle of peppermint schnapps in the other.

I jumped up and said, "Oh, no, you don't! Put that bottle away for now. We can't afford to let a gallon of cheap liquor dull our funny bones and our chances of—"

"—knocking the knickers off Aliyah!" Justin interrupted.

Tim understood. He put the bottle under the kitchen sink and said, "I can pour it down the drain if you think it's too tempting here."

I jumped up. "No! That will be our reward after we're finished." We all smiled that I-can-hardly-wait-to-get-buzzed-beyond-belief-on-peppermint-schnapps smile.

We finally finished reworking the set at one thirty in the morning. Actually, we threw out all the jokes and built a completely new set. Even though I was groggy with exhaustion, I stood up to deliver the set to Justin, who had wandered into the kitchen and was pouring himself a glass of that yummy peppermint liquor, and a now-sleeping Tim.

"Did you know that Jesus was into CrossFit? It's true. His favorite shoes were Cross-trainers." A thumbs up from Justin, still in the kitchen. "I was looking at the newspaper ads and got excited because my local supermarket was having a blow-out sale on birthday cake candles.

"What do creatures in the ocean put on their front door at Christmas time? A reef." Another thumbs up.

"I met a woman who didn't like cars. She wanted nothing to do with them. In fact, they made her ill if she got in one. She had an autoimmune disease." Justin settled back on the couch. Tim was still sleeping.

"My high school math teacher fell in love with a cow. He brought her home to his parents and introduced her.

'Mom, Dad, this is my significant udder.' Speaking of cows, a married cow couple got a divorce. The lawyer decided that the mom cow would have the kids every udder weekend." Justin was grinning.

"Did you see this on the news? Trixie the pig fell and scraped her knee. Her mom treated the injury with first aid oinkment. Where does one send used cat litter? To a PU box. Speaking of animals, I walked into a bar full of people watching a horse race on TV. I asked, 'Who's whinny-ing?'" Tim was still sleeping.

"My friend Rochelle the duck likes to jog on hot summer days. She never leaves home without her waddle bottle." Justin was laughing now.

"Did you hear about my sister-in-law, Elaine? She's an engineer with an advanced degree in the science of testing water for alkalinity or acidity. She has a pH in chemistry. And finally, let me tell you about my friend Mark." I decided to include one of the jokes I had told Justin when I first met him. "He's one of the world's leading specialists at helping people get items off their floors and up onto accessible platforms in order to organize their homes. He's a shelf-help guru."

I sat down in silence as Justin handed me a glass of schnapps. "That one is still funny!" We clinked glasses as he said, "I think we have a winner here."

Tim woke up. "I was actually awake the whole time. This set is so good, I was silently crying with pride. You will surely light Aliyah's fire!"

※ ※ ※

On the appointed day and time, I drove alone to my second audition. I wanted to mentally prepare and didn't want Tim or Justin to bother or influence me.

Upon entering the building, I was directed by an impossibly good-looking young man to step into a waiting room of sorts. Four other people were there, three men and a woman. Through the wall, we could faintly hear the current auditionee presenting her routine. After a few minutes she stopped. We could hear some mumbling, obviously typical post-audition chatter, something like, "Thank you, we will be in touch if you are selected."

Then we could hear a male voice, louder and clearer than the woman's, begin telling a joke. As he told a joke, I realized the voice was familiar. Wait. Oh my goodness! It was Justin! What the freakin' frick was he doing here?

"My father was a mountain climber. He saw a tall, hairy creature in the Himalayan region of Nepal and saw that the creature had amazing stomach muscles. It was known as the Abdominal Snowman." Holy theft! That was *my* joke!

"When my son was a teenager, he really disliked washing dishes. My wife and I couldn't understand why until one day my wife picked up the container of dishwashing soap and noticed we had purchased the wrong product. It was Dishwashing *Deterrent.*"

I sat there with my mouth hanging open. I looked around the room at the others and felt compelled to explain what was going on, but then reconsidered. It would make me look foolish to admit that my writing partner was stabbing me in the back.

"My brother receives all his correspondence electronically. He gets super-frustrated because whenever he sends a letter, it gets destroyed. Whenever he receives a letter it arrives destroyed. He finally figured out he was using e-maul." *Another* joke that I helped Justin write!

I couldn't keep it to myself. I had to share with the people in the waiting room, but I made it look like I knew about his audition. "That's my writing partner in there. We wrote that one together," I said proudly. The people in the room smiled at me.

We heard Justin exchange formalities with another person, then silence. It felt like an hour, but finally the pretty young man came into the room and asked us all to come through the door and be ready to give our auditions. We were seated in the audience, and Aliyah was sitting there, too. It was weird watching the others audition, but it really boosted my confidence. I noticed all the strengths and, more importantly, the flaws in each person's routine.

When the announcer called my name, all my tummy butterflies had flown. I bounded up to the stage and got right to it. I launched into the set we had worked so hard on together.

Aliyah smiled and even laughed during the routine. When I finished, they shouted out, "Keep going!"

"Oh, um, okay! President Teddy Roosevelt was thrilled when the Panama Canal was completed. He asked his buddy Irving Berlin to write a song for the opening ceremony. Irving was working on a Christmas song at the time, but rewrote the lyrics for his friend Teddy: 'I'm dreaming of a wide isthmus, and may all your isthmuses be wide.'"

Aliyah was still laughing. "More!"

"Ralph the plumber is interested in tango, monster trucks, vegetarian cooking, baseball, astrology, bird watching, and heavy metal music. He's multi-fauceted. My seamstress is prone to arguing. Outside her shop window the sign reads 'Altercations While You Wait.'"

Aliyah and their assistants were smiling and laughing at all of my jokes. I forgot all about trying to end my set perfectly and just rattled off every joke that came to mind.

"My neighbor assists in home childbirth. One day there was a big scheduling conflict and birthing complications. She had a midwife crisis. My old high school auto shop teacher was addicted to smelling paint fumes. His doctor ordered him to quit. Now he's suffering from wiffdrawls. Maxi the Mouse had a minimum wage job. She eeked out a living."

Aliyah was cracking up. "Kirsten, my cheeks and abs hurt from laughing! Oh, gosh, gimme a break!" They stood up with a big grin, clapping. "Thanks for the great set and all the bonus jokes!" they said.

I walked into the waiting area. Everyone was gone, so I let myself out and drove home.

* * *

I lingered, loitered, and lazed for five days on a lemon-yellow davenport in our apartment while I sucked on lime-and-loganberry-flavored lollies. I could hardly eat or sleep. Five anxious days without a word from Aliyah's people. Five twenty-four-hour cycles of waking, lazing, sleeping, and being vaguely aware of Tim's coming and going.

    I finally assumed that I hadn't been chosen and avoided talking about it with everyone who knew I had auditioned for Aliyah's sidekick role. One thing that was nibbling away at me was the issue of Justin secretly auditioning for the same job. Although I hadn't known him very long, I thought I had picked up a strong vibe of honesty and loyalty. He's been rock steady and sweet to me. I admit that I've had thoughts of us being more than writing partners. To be perfectly honest, I've fantasized about having intimate relations with him in a wheelbarrow on a construction site, on the hood of an old rusty truck, on the floor in an auto repair shop (while his manly hands smear me with grease), and in the dusty, uncomfortable awkwardness of a parking garage stairwell. You know, typical places that women prefer to engage in lovemaking.

    But now, knowing that he sneaked into the audition without telling me, I was floundering in chagrin, disconcert, and perturbation. I locked myself in my room for twenty-four hours, ate fourteen pints of Ben and Jerry's Cookies and Cream Cheesecake ice cream, and watched hundreds of precious, funny cat compilation videos.

    I awoke from an afternoon nap upon hearing Tim clank and clunk in the kitchen. His food prep abilities are nil. He says he'd rather take a multivitamin pill than learn to cook. I sat upright and said, "Tim, old buddy, old pal, what are we doing here, anyway?"

    He replied, "You mean to say what are *you* doing here, anyway? Because I know why *I'm* here."

"Well, lucky *you* for knowing your purpose. Okay, what am *I* doing here anyway?"

"Hey," he smiled. "That's a cool title for a song."

I said, "It's already a song, but regardless of that, what am I *actually* doing here? I mean, on planet Earth?"

"First tell me about the song," Tim said.

"It's cool and up tempo. It has a great bass riff and fun, thought-provoking lyrics. I bet you'd love it. It's by our friend Lucky Doug Fergus's band."

"Ooh! I love Lucky Doug Fergus's quirky songs and voice."

"Dig this, Timster, on the recorded version (available on all digital platforms), the lead vocal is sung by our friend Greg Scarborough!"

Tim jumped and clapped his hands, "Goodie! The ol' Gregster! I'll stream it tonight!"

"That's nice of you, but can we get back to me and my feeling of hopelessness?"

Tim walked from the kitchen toward me. "Here's my best advice, which I got from someone on the internet: live each day as if it were your last."

I stared at him. "Really? You mean I should max out all three of my credit cards on yoga retreats and twelve pallets of knitting yarn? Then eat four gallons of organic vanilla/coconut/sardine ice cream and drink myself silly on twenty-six bottles of paprika/lime-flavored non-alcoholic cream soda?"

"Now Kirsten, that was a lame, ludicrous, and loquacious elucidation."

"But Tim, it's ridiculous when people say to live as if it were your last day." Especially when I feel hopeless.

Hmmm, let's see. Feeling hopeless on my last day, I'd probably pull the frickin' plug *before* the end of the day!"

"Oh, honey, I'm sorry. Don't feel hopeless! You're still in the running to be the sidekick for one of the biggest celebrities in Hollywood!"

I exhaled loudly and fell back, supine, on the couch. "Oh, I know you're right, but after five days of waiting, *and* knowing that my boyfriend stabbed me in the back—"

"*—boyfriend?*" Tim cut in.

"Oops. I didn't mean to say that. But the fact is, I've been getting along so easily with him lately. Well, I was *before* the audition. Am I wrong to think that he could someday be my boyfriend? It seems I've lost momentum, and something feels weird now. When the frick will Aliyah's people call?! Why hasn't there been a single peep from Justin?!"

Tim calmly said, "I can't answer that. What does he do with himself when he's not with us working on our comedy?"

"You know, that's a great question. I don't know. I guess I don't really know him all that well." Tim remained silent. I continued, "My mind just goes to the worst place."

He said, "I hear you saying that your mind goes to the worst place. You probably think that Aliyah believes you're a talentless dork and Justin only used you to get his foot in Aliyah's door, right?"

I said, "Do you think so?"

He snapped, "Kirsten! No! I *don't* think so. I was just surmising ironically, like sitcom characters do!" I told him I was sorry. "Don't apologize, but please know that you, more than any person I know, have a purpose, a destiny. I even wrote a poem for you last night."

"Really? For your sister?"

"Yes. Here it is. 'A teabag lives for the day it gets boiled. The salmon can't wait for the day it gets broiled. The river loved foam and dreamed it was roiled. An airplane wing sings on the day it gets foiled. My reputation can't wait for the day it gets soiled. My garden hose proposed to me on the day it got coiled.'"

"Oh, Timster! I love it! Thank you. I agree; I *do* have a purpose."

"Are you sure?"

"Yes! I do. I do! I DO!"

He smiled. "And if you lived in the ocean . . ."

I blurted out, "I would have a *porpoise*!" We both guffawed unrestrainedly over that one.

Just then a text came in on my phone—from Justin. Then it rang. It was Aliyah's manager! It could be good news or bad. Yikes! I calmed my nerves by going to the worst possible scenarios: Justin wants to stop working with me and has no romantic interest whatsoever. Aliyah's manager is going to pass on me and wish me good luck in my future enterprises.

***

It wasn't bad news. I sit here now, on this lovely, breezy porch, sixty-seven years after that fateful day. I like to look across the street at the house that's occupied by a young family of four as they come and go in a rush. Both parents work long hours, and the kids are in constant motion with sports, music, and drama classes. I envy them. I well remember those days. I did have a wonderful forty-five years with my Justin before someone's higher power decided he was needed *up there* more than he was needed *down here*. Our kids and grandkids visit when they can. I've lived a blessed life. I still live on my royalties from twenty-two years on network TV as Aliyah's sidekick. God, I loved her. I mean him. I mean—oh, dang it.

AMERICA'S GOT MEDIOCRITY

Announcer: It's time for America's favorite television show, America's Got Mediocrity! I'm your host, Luke Warm. How is everyone doing tonight? I'm feeling just okay, and I hope you are, too. I don't know; I guess we should get started.

Our first participant is Molly Medium. She has no real story to tell and has never struggled or been deprived of any basic necessity. Molly is from a wonderful family. Her parents adored her and gave her lots of love and encouragement, but they didn't overdo it or push her too much. All four of her grandparents are still alive and email her regularly to check in and let her know that they love her.

It's incredible that Molly has come so far on her journey without the impetus of psychological damage to push her along. She's a solid C student in school. She can make banana muffins. She sewed her two Girl Scout badges—one for being mostly prompt to meetings and one for completing her three-mile jog/walk in less than four hours—on her uniform all by herself.

Molly is fourteen and still can't ride a bike very well, but one of her skills is the ability to recall from memory three names of past United States presidents. Oh, I should add that she can sometimes score a run during a softball game.

Here on America's Got Mediocrity, the performances are rated from zero to ten, with ten, of course, being the highest score. As in the Olympics, after a performance, the judges will hold up a scorecard with a number that they feel represents that performer's level of excellence. But here on America's Got Mediocrity, the judges' scorecards only go from four to six. Let's get started.

Molly Medium, please take the stage and introduce yourself to the panel.

Molly: Hello. I'm Molly Medium. I'm here today to show you my skill of standing on one foot while talking. In fact, I'm doing it now. (Audience claps half-heartedly.)

Announcer: Judges, please hold up your score cards. Okay, nice. All four judges have given Molly a solid five. Well, that's the end of our show. I don't know if you will be able to tune in next week, but if you can't, no biggie. Until next time, goodbye from all of us here at America's Got Mediocrity.

EARN AS YOU LEARN

Like many people, I needed money. I liked working, but I was ready to move on from my current job. Thankfully, I had time to contemplate the many employment options that were available to me. As a thirty-three-year-old high school graduate who had pulled weeds, washed dishes, dug ditches, cut firewood, and swept the floors of metal-fabrication shops, I knew that I was just coming into my prime. Soon I would be riding life in style, wearing a toothy golden smile, living eighteen floors up, drinking from a silver cup, certain that I would be clinking a glass with members of the ruling class.

I had the safety net of working for a company that made industrial telephone cable assemblies. They loved me, and my continuous employment was a given. It wasn't bad work, but I didn't think it was my reason for occupying the planet. I worked with the maintenance crew, changing light bulbs, waxing floors, emptying waste receptacles, and such. My specialty was the daily assignment of using needle-nose pliers to pluck cigarette butts out of the screens in the men's room urinals.

Tasks that required special knowledge or experience were off limits to us lowly building sanitation and maintenance engineers. A specialty contractor had to be called in when a problem arose with the plumbing, electrical, or heating/air conditioning systems.

When a highly trained and experienced expert was on site attending to a problem, I would slink quietly to a vantage point just out of sight of the tech and affect a pose of mock indifference. As I stared at their side-slung belt and the bulging tool pouch at their hips, I couldn't help but feel mild envy at their expertise in using the various screwdrivers, test devices, and specialty gear. When the specialist had solved the brain teaser and the system was back online, I would step out from my covert vantage point and say, "Was it the reversible pulse-phase ratcheting submerger?" The tech would give a highly simplified explanation, as if speaking to a child. I would mumble "mmm hmmm" a couple of times with detached interest, then slowly turn and walk away. I wouldn't give the tech the satisfaction of thinking I was actually interested.

During my lunch breaks, I would amble to Larry's Liquor Lair, the fine beverage and snack establishment next door, and buy hotdogs and a bottle of delicious, piquant, utterly ambrosial Boone's Farm Strawberry Hill wine (with overtones of sweaty teenagers and motorcycle racetracks). I'd spend the rest of my thirty-minute lunchtime out in the parking lot, sitting in my truck, nibbling elegantly on the hotdogs from the warming machine, where the frankfurters had been rotating around and around for three days prior to my purchase. I'd take delicate sips of the Boone's Farm *vino de fresas* while reading my trade copy of Telephone Cable Assembly Is the Most Fascinating Career *Ever*.

As I imbibed and masticated, I listened to the failed and frustrated wannabe entertainer and politician Lunk Limbrogan's AM talk radio show. Lunk had gathered a huge audience from his skillful delivery of skewed political information, fabrications, and outright lies. He knew his listeners were typically male, twenty-five to fifty-five years old, and drove primer-gray pickup trucks with lift kits and oversized tires. Surprisingly, however, many of his most fanatical listeners were women.

Lunks's doltish devotees preferred hate and anger to happiness, so he stealthily fed them what they wanted to hear. His fans tuned in by the primer-gray truckload, which made him a millionaire from the advertising revenue. Of course, I wasn't one of those types. I listened only to try to understand the minds of those who concurred with Mr. Limbrogan's ideology. I assure you that listening to Lunk Limbrogan's radio show would never persuade me to slide across the line from the light side of seeking a happy view of life to the dark side of finding satisfaction in hating someone or something. Oh. Now that I think about it, the doors on my truck *are* primer gray. (While I was sitting in my truck reading, listening, and eating, I suddenly thought, why do we wolf *down* but gobble *up* food?)

As I said, I wasn't averse to working, but lately, while on duty at the factory, I had been daydreaming of getting a new job, something off the well-worn trail. I know what you're thinking. *Does anyone actually* want *to work anymore? It seems that no one wants a job in 2023, unless they can work from home.* I hear you, reader. Currently in America, there are Help Wanted signs in front of nearly every business in cities and towns across the country. Employers can hardly find workers at all, let alone quality labor. There is even a trend where employers are offering a signing bonus (similar to the professional sports industry) to prospective employees to lure people to apply.

Burger Czar is hiring! A one-thousand-dollar bonus to qualified hirees! Starting pay is $54.50 per hour! A free meal and one snack for each four-hour shift! Free child care and pet sitting! Don't feel like coming in today? Don't! Stay home and play video games in your underwear, practice guitar, or sleep till 1:00, then order pizza for breakfast. We'll see you when you feel like coming in again.

And this from the national hardware store chain Doohickeys for Your Habitat:

All employees have daily access to the shooting range and dirt bike track on our property for your practice and fun. We provide the guns and bikes! While working in the store, we encourage you to keep your phone in one hand at all times. We know how important it is to stay connected to your social media followers and to quickly answer when a spouse, partner, friend, or child calls with urgent communication, such as, "Did you see that video of the cat walking on a piano keyboard?!"

This apathy toward work is very strange, especially considering America was built on people working like crazy to achieve their respective American dreams. There surely used to be a subliminal brainwashing program that made people crave working. Ninety-five percent of Americans seem programmed at birth to have one purpose: Finish school so that they can work five days a week, all year every year, with two weeks off per year, for forty years straight in order to afford a house, a washing machine, a large-screen TV, video games, an automobile, and a four-burner propane outdoor barbeque grill.

The other five percent who avoid this work-to-death mentality are ridiculed as lazy, no good leeches. But why, how, and when did civilization become all about work, work, work? And who was the dingleberry brain who invented the five-day work week with only two days off? Why not a two-day work week with five days off?

(The fun and talented music artist Lucky Doug Fergus wrote this lyric for his song "Five Day Weekend," available on all digital music outlets: "I got a job so I could buy a car, so I could get to work to pay it off.")

Most of the employees at the telephone cable assembly factory were sweet Hispanic ladies who sat and operated machines that took the many tiny wires at the ends of long cables and inserted each wire into a brass connector. I was well liked (it seemed) by the ladies. I knew very little Spanish (*se muy poco español*), but I attempted to converse with them, and I think it endeared me to them. I would say things like, "*A mi tortuga mascota le encanta comer sándwiches de fresa y sardina*" (my pet turtle loves to eat strawberry and sardine sandwiches). The ladies would giggle politely. I think their maternal instincts kicked in when they looked at me because I was tall and thin and they felt I needed fattening up. When I looked into their eyes, I could sense them wishing to have me over for dinner and feed me plates of *tacos al pastor con arroz y frijoles con queso*.

I was ready to start a new career, and I didn't care about a silly signing bonus. Maybe a *singing* bonus. Yes, I believe I would work for a company that gave me a monetary perk for allowing me to belt out classic fifteenth century smooth-opera songs on duty.

I sometimes wondered if I could be paid for being thin. Could I find a way to receive compensation for being a slim, average-looking, goofy, somewhat immature, fairly unevolved thirty-three-year-old man-child? Yes, I desired to be remunerated for my physicality. (Isn't remunerated just a fancy way of saying *paid*? And shouldn't it be re*num*erated, pronounced *re-noo-merated*? I mean, it's referring to numbers. *Noom*-erals and *num*-bers, not *moon*-erals and *mun*-bers.)

As I was saying, I wanted to be recompensed for my physicality. I took a long, lingering look at my lean, lanky, lithe self in the looking glass. I liked what I saw, but I had to admit I was not quite there, so I made some changes to my clothes and hair. I quit my job at the factory and said "*Adiós*, dulces damas. Espero que todos tengan vidas maravillosamente largas." (Goodbye, sweet ladies. I hope you all have wonderfully long lives.)

On my way home I stopped in at a Nothing Wholesome or Nutritious Here convenience market to pick up an old-fashioned local help-wanted paper. Once I was back to the cozy safety of my sweet domicile—a converted plywood tool shed attached to my parents garage—I sank into my stinky, decrepit, barf-yellow easy chair and began to peruse the *ayuda quería papel* (help wanted paper).

I narrowed my eyelids, like that famous actor who played tough guys in the movies, Squint Eastwood, scanning for any mention of physical attributes in the title of each ad. Surely I could find an employer who was seeking the specimen of a tall, thin, thirty-three-year-old male.

By default, my gaze fell naturally upon words that indicated manual labor jobs: shoveling, chopping, carrying, and lifting. I noticed an entire category called Unskilled Labor. Wait a gosh-darn sixtieth of an hour! I'm not unskilled! I have more than a decade of experience in several labor disciplines. Unskilled, my eye. If there were a TV show called America's Got Skills, I'd be the big winner after my fabulous demonstrations of pulling weeds, washing dishes, digging ditches, cutting firewood, and sweeping floors.

As I continued to scan, I started losing hope and feeling bad when my eyes fell upon the ad titled, *Young man wanted to make me feel glad*. I called the number, and we made a date. She said, "Come right over. Don't hesitate. You can earn as you learn, oh yes, earn as you learn!" I drove swiftly and somewhat recklessly to the address she had provided. I found her driveway, rolled up, and the guard on duty waved me in.

Following her instructions, I walked around to the

backdoor/laundry room entrance and opened it, wearing a grin. My eyes popped out, cartoon-like, at the inconceivable beauty standing next to her washer and dryer. She had everything any human could possibly want—except me (and maybe one of those trendy new air fryers). She was hypnotically alluring and appeared to be twice my age.

She said, "I'm ravenous for a multi-course meal. Won't you release me from my cage?"

I could feel my fortitude quickly dissipating. Could it be that I was out of my league? I said, "Oh, gosh, I'd like to help you, but I don't have commensurate experience. Maybe I'll just go back."

She quickly replied, "Oh, no, no, no! You're already here! You can earn as you learn!"

"Of course." I smiled nervously as I tried to hang on to my as-yet-unproven playboy reputation."

Come to my room," she said buoyantly. "Let's play a game!"

Coyly I replied, "Maybe later. Oh! I just remembered that my cat is having a shampoo today at the pet groomer!"

She said with a sudden cool demeanor, "I don't believe it. Remember that I'm paying for this."

I timidly admitted, "You're right, I know. I'm Sorry."

Well, great gosh almighty, my life story came out in a flash. Soon she taught me some new tricks and I learned that yes, one can earn as one learns.

*   *   *

Months rolled on by like a tattooed, baggy-panted, Ocean Spray Cran-Apple-guzzling slacker skateboarder drifting down a gentle, paved slope while the mellow sounds of Fleetwood Mac wafted from the smartphone in her back pocket.

I was getting to know my affable friend better and better with each session. I was certain now that someday we would be a congenial, convivial, companionable, congruous couple. I contemplated all the ways I would approach presenting a proposal to my hypnotically alluring, inconceivable beauty (HAIB). I was confident that she would be agreeable to my concept of cohabitation in a community of commingled shipping containers. I practiced my prepared speech silently in my head as I got up from my bed in the plywood lean-to at my parents' abode. I was flush with a new virile poise that would speak volumes without making any noise. Now, at thirty-three years old, I was finally ready to leave my bachelorhood. I knew she loved me; she said I'm good!

"Oh boy!" I said aloud as I drove on a cloud with happy butterflies in my tummy. Then, a momentary pause, as I couldn't recall whether she liked Go Fish or Gin Rummy. "No matter; that's trivial," I said to placate my troops. Then I couldn't recall; did her lobes like dangles or hoops?

I arrived with a wink and a nod from the guard and noticed a particular brilliance from the flora in the yard. I flung open the door and rushed inside. The fact that I hadn't called first surprised her, which injured my pride. I said to her, with all the pretentious presumptuousness of an inordinately hyped pop star, "Let's move away! We'll find a house in the country where we can both play. We'll adopt cats and rats and elephants and sure as you're born, we'll find ourselves a bass-playing, windsurfing, vegan unicorn!"

She replied by shaking her head side to side and began a long, slow *uuuuummmm*. I was instantly crushed like a tomato at her less-than-yes response. She said, "Easy, tiger. Now let me explain. I want your love, but only when I call. Let's not get in too deep and spoil it all. But you can earn as you learn, oh yes, earn as you learn!"

I couldn't see continuing the relationship only for physical pleasure. I had tasted the tip of my HAIB's iceberg (and oh boy, what an iceberg it was!). I wanted more than just chips and salsa. I wanted the whole chimichanga with her: Love and trust. Laughing and sharing our most intimate secrets. The comfort to fart in each other's presence. Taking long, candle-lit walks on the beach. Reading chapters of a Haynes 1975 Ford Pinto repair manual to each other while soaking in a bubble bath. Grappling over why I couldn't remember to enter purchases into our joint checking account register book. Arguing over why she would insist on using this old-fashioned method of tracking when I would keep telling her that all banking can be done online now.

What had started out as a new and exciting career change soon became something much bigger, richer, and more delicious than simply being a gigolo. Meeting my HAIB was undeniable fate. It was destiny, predetermination, inevitability, kismet, and other names for exotic dancers. After my attempt at being a paid man-about-town, I had assumed that the universe would have recognized my sudden and deep commitment to my HAIB and would've protected, nurtured, and prolonged the relationship to eternity and beyond, but now she was gone. There were moments when I was weak and wanted only to experience her carnal delights (and I could have used a little dough, dinero, and coinage), but she emphatically emphasized (without a hint of emphysema) that she didn't want to be roped and tied, altar-bound and hypnotized. She wanted the soothing sounds of sweet freedom to remain whispering in her ears.

What had gone wrong with my HAIB? Maybe our senses of humor were not in alignment. I had fabricated a joke for her, but she hadn't laughed. Maybe that was a sign. Oh, my HAIB. My dear, delightful, hypnotically alluring, inconceivable beauty was a gift that appeared in my world at the right time. I suppose some gifts can't (or shouldn't) be kept, but instead set free to continue giving to others.

For a time, I couldn't imagine life without her—but that was *months* ago. I've evolved and grown since then. Yet I'm still slowly healing from the breakup with her. It's been three months, and I still have a slight ache in the left side of my chest, but it's fading fast. (I appreciate you for feeling my pain with me. Thank you. Go ahead and donate some sum of money to your favorite charity in memory of my heartache. [My lovely reader, I just improvised that line. It took all of five seconds to write it. It just poured out of me: *Go ahead and donate some sum of money to your favorite charity in memory of my heartache.* Should I send it to Nashville and see if any country music people want it?])

* * *

I decided to ingest my pride and go back to the telephone cable factory to see if I could get my job back. First, I made sure that Larry's Liquor Lair was still in business so that I could quickly source my delicious, piquant, utterly ambrosial Boone's Farm Strawberry Hill wine and the rotating frankfurters.

I scheduled a meeting with the president of the company, Karizzma Chizzel. She was known as a tough but fair leader of the company. I was somewhat afraid of her.

I told her, "In truth, Miss Chizzel, I never did mind changing light bulbs, waxing floors, emptying waste receptacles, and such. I actually like picking cigarette butts out of urinal screens. Am I weird?" I chuckled.

"Yes, that is weird," Karizzma said, matter-of-factly.

I continued, "It appeals to my mild case of obsessive/compulsive disorder. It's like the gratification I get when I successfully pluck diseased bones and organs out of the body on that board game, Operation." I smiled.

"So, you still play Operation?" asked Karizzma.

"Um, well... yes. Sometimes. Not often, really," I said with an embarrassed, crooked smile.

She smiled back. "Well, I like that you do. My great-grandfather invented that game, and my trust fund still gets royalty payments whenever a game is purchased."

"Really!? Wow, that is super cool!" I nervously and over-excitedly bellowed.

"Actually, no. I was having a bit of fun with you. My

great-grandfather was a garbage truck driver for the lovely city of Inkster, Michigan. He hauled the trash for thirty-seven years, but he never invented anything—unless you consider his technique of cutting open a nearly empty toothpaste tube with scissors in order to scrape out every last bit of paste an invention."

She went on, "I've been thinking of making our brand more prominent in the public's eye. No one really knows or cares who makes their telephone cables and connectors. But I want to position us to eventually be the most famous telephone cable manufacturer in the country so that one day I can sell this giant headache for a huge pile of ducats. Do you dig me, Dougie?" I smiled and nodded.

"I think you could be our company mascot. You're tall and wiry." Then she yelled, "We'll call you *Wirey!*" My mouth dropped open in amazement that she would consider me for such an unusual purpose.

I suddenly grinned a football field wide. "I love that idea! I had been debating whether to apply to be an apprentice owl trainer at the zoo or return here to work. I'm now ecstatically exultant that I chose to return here!"

"Did you just say *ecstatically exultant?*"

"Um . . . yes?" I tentatively answered.

"Oh, Dougie!" she blurted. "You are definitely not the average cigarette butt plucker!"

"Thank you, Karizzma. I mean, Miss Chizzel. You are definitely the brains of this company. I see us having a scintillating, glistening, glittering, glowing future. Of course, I'm talking about the future of the *company*, not you and me personally."

"Oh, really, Dougie?" She threw a seductive smile my way. "Did you just say *scintillating* and *glistening*?"

"Um... yes?"

"Oh, Dougie, I never knew this about you. I thought you were just one of our bland, boorish maintenance workers with a fetish for urine-soaked cigarette butts." I smiled proudly.

She continued. "Let me brain-blizzard this whole concept of hiring you as our company's representative. In the meanwhile, I don't want you stuck working in maintenance. I need you as our new mascot. Hmmm." She tapped her long, glue-on fingernails on her desktop. "I have an idea. My bland and boorish ex-husband abandoned several cars in our barn. He left them to rot, like he did me." Her lower lip started to quiver. "They all need work so that I can sell them for top dollar."

I jumped up from my chair. "Oh, Miss Chizzel, please don't cry." She fought back tears. "That idiot ex-husband of yours is the biggest loser *ever*!"

"Oh, Dougie, call me Karizzma. And . . . thank you. You're the sweetest company mascot *ever*! In fact, I'm going to start calling you by your mascot name, Wirey." Cheered up now, she said, "Let's go out to my place so I can show you those clunkers. When you're not doing mascot work, you can stay with me and fix them!"

"All right, Karizzma, but I don't know a thing about being a mascot, and I've never done so much as put air in the tires of a car."

She chuckled. "Wirey, you silly savage. Don't you know? You can earn as you learn!"

"All right, but I have to tell you that I've never lived with a CEO of a company."

"Don't be presumptuous, Wirey. You won't be living *with* me. You'll be living *at* my place." She winked. "I might ask you to bring in a bucket of coal for the heating system. Can you carry out that task?"

I stuttered, "I—I—I've never done that before."

"And I may ask you to sweep out my basement. Can you handle that?"

"I—I—I've never done that before, either."

"And I may ask you to pump water from the well. Can you leverage that situation?"

"I—I—I've never done that before, either."

"Now, Wirey, you needn't fret that you ain't done much of anything yet. I'll teach you, dig me? You can—" We simultaneously blurted out, "—earn as you learn!"

* * *

Life has been one merrymaking moment after another living at my boss's house. She's really funny. She explodes—I mean *exudes*—joy. Who knew? She's all business at the cable factory, but at home she's an all-you-can-eat buffoon. If she had a music group, it would be called Karizzma Jokester and the Cards.

After I got all the cars running (thanks to instructional videos on YouTube) and sold, there wasn't much to do at her property. It was then that she suggested I could earn a little extra money by selling products from her side business. I was agreeable to that notion. I wanted to show her I was sailing with a cargo full of love and devotion. In truth, I was seeing her in a new light: not just a CEO anymore, she was becoming a potential life partner.

I know what you're thinking, dear reader. You're thinking I have a hankering for older, financially secure women. But that's *not* it. It's much broader than that. Come on, give me some acknowledgment that it's possible I could have grown beyond being a cheap-wine-sipping, rancid-hot-dog-nibbling factory worker. Okay, then, will you please give me some credit for wanting to improve my life, even if it's by attaching to the coattails of others? The fact that the others are female and have more money than I do should have no bearing on this discussion. What? Oh, right. I see. I hear you saying that the fact that the others are female and have more money than I do is exactly the point. All right, enough dragging me over the coals. Let's move on.

One morning Karizzma walked from the main house to the guest house to wake me up and tell me something. She had enrolled me in a training class to learn how to sell her company's products. With the name AmBioLifeNutriWakeTech, I felt it would be easy to sell the various creams, pills, and powders that were scientifically rumored to improve your eyesight, remove grime from any surface, increase your car's gas mileage, purge your bowels, and add ears to your life. There was a momentary hiccup in AmBioLifeNutriWakeTech's trajectory when they had to battle a class-action lawsuit over the misprint "add *ears* to your life" in all of the promotional materials. Thousands of people claimed they never grew any more auricles after consuming the product.

I wouldn't have predicted that I could sell stuff, but man-o-man could I sell! I could hustle and hawk-like a pimpin' bird. I was selling so much that I had to recruit every friend, acquaintance, and cousin to sell for me. When I needed more help, I approached strangers at the gym, on the bus, in the park, and while cruising those nearly obsolete shopping malls, where I practiced my speed walking with all of the blue- and gray-haired retirees.

One morning Karizzma and I woke up. (Yes, we were now sleeping in the same bed.) She said, "Holy wow, Dougie! Look at this email from my accountant. Your talent at moving merchandise is keeping the telephone cable assembly business ringing!

× × ×

On the afternoon of an October full moon, I was marveling about my amazing new life. I decided to inform Karizzma that it was time for us to publicly reveal that we were a couple. At the same moment, I got a text from her: *Come to office ASAP. Our geese R cooked! Big bummer. Hurry!*

When I walked in, Karizzma was pacing back and forth behind her desk and mumbling intelligibly. I cried out, "Honey, what is it?"

She snapped at me, "Shut the door! And don't call me *honey!*"

"All right, what is going on?"

"We've been found out! The Feds are shutting down AmBioLifeNutriWakeTech, and you are likely going to have to get some cast-iron underwear." I couldn't comprehend her, and she knew it. "Look, Dougie dippy. You might be on your way to prison. You were too good at recruiting people to sell my products. The Feds found out and have deemed that you were operating a pyramid scheme."

"What do you mean, *I* was operating it?"

"Listen, Dougie dippy, my little side business flew under the radar before you got involved and blew it up into a million-dollar-a-month operation! I assume you wanted that and liked the extra income. *I'm* certainly not going to prison!"

"First of all," I said, "I didn't calculate any of it. It just sort of happened that the sales kept going up and up. But when I saw how well I was doing, then yes, I became driven to do more because I love you and want us to be life partners and I thought it would make you love me more!"

Shaking her head, she said, "Dougie, Dougie, Dougie. No, no, no. We were just having fun, you dippity-do. Remember, *earn as you learn*?" I was instantly deflated and felt nauseated. She continued, "I'm sure you'll find a life partner in prison." Then she smirked. "It may be a Bubba or a Roscoe or an Otis, but by golly, I think he's waitin' there fer ya."

Karizzma was only half correct. I did meet my life partner in prison, just not the romantic kind. Virgil is my business partner. One sunny day out in the yard I was doing masticatorii lateral fly press-jumps with seventy-five-pound dumbbells when Virgil cautiously approached me and said, "Bro, do you even lift?" I cracked up and dropped a dumbbell on my left foot. We became fast friends and vowed to better our lives when we got out.

"I think we should capitalize on what we're already good at," Virgil said.

"Virgie, baby, the gramma-mattingly correct way to say that is, *I think we should capitalize on what that which we are at which already good*," I corrected.

"Ok, Dougie. I trust you to be my gramma-mattingly advisor."

"Thanks, Virgie. Now tell me again about your idea for capital-eye-zing on our strengths."

"Okay, but stand back a bit, 'cause when I get excited my eyes bug out, I flail my arms, and I spray cornucopian amounts of saliva into the air," he warned. I stepped back three paces and braced for a sprinkling on my face. He said, "There is one activity that we both *love* to do, and I think we ought to get paid to do it!"

I guessed, "Masticatorii lateral fly press-jumps?"

"Oh, right, I forgot that we both love those. But no, Dougie. Remember the day we both had latrine duty and admitted to each other that we actually love—" I cut in and completed his sentence. "—picking cigarette butts out of urinal screens!" Virgil jumped up and shouted, "Yes!"

* * *

I got out after four years of good behavior. My masticatorii muscles had gotten huge from forty-eight months of following the online advice of six-time Mr. Olympia

Dorian Yates and doing those lateral fly press-jumps. Virgil got out soon after me, but he almost got held back and punished. On the day he was released, Virgil was so joyful that as he was walking out, he started chanting, "I'm gettin' out today! I'm gettin' out today!" As he passed by a guard, Virgil suddenly jumped up and kissed him on the lips. At first, the guard was furious and called the warden to file a complaint. Then Virgil smiled and hollered, "I kissed a guard and I liked it!" Everyone within ear shot laughed.

We soon started our business servicing commercial and industrial restrooms. V & D Cig Butt Pluckers, LLC, is now the biggest cigarette butt removal company in our tri-county region. We proudly employ only ex-convicts. We keep growing, adding more commercial and industrial customers and hiring more ex-cons. We ask each new hire if they have done this kind of work before. When they answer no, we tell them, "It's okay! *You can earn as you learn!*"

ACKNOWLEDGMENTS

I want to thank my wife, Suzan Beraza, and the many family members who encouraged me to keep going, finish my book, and told me that my writing is in some small way a positive contribution to society.

Thank you and a tip of my newsboy cap to my team of readers who checked for typographical errors and shared their reviews: Susan, Jay, Mark, Felicity, Russ, Anita, Bob, Elaine, and Nick.

Finally, big thanks and a hearty *hip-hip huzzah*! to my editor, Jessica Vineyard, my book designer, Christy Day, and my book marketing coach, Martha Bullen.

And to you, dear reader, for taking precious time out of your life to read this book! I'm flattered and humbled. Thank you!

ABOUT THE AUTHOR

DOUGLAS FERGUS (aka Doug) is the author of more than one hundred…I mean, more than *one* book. *Quit Honking! (I'm Pedaling as Fast as I Can)* is his second book.

Doug and his family dwelled in sunny California during the groovy 1960s in his hometown of Sierra Madre. His maternal grandfather was a pun and joke lover who cultivated Doug's habit of noticing the absurd and ridiculous in everyday life.

Early on, Doug developed a fascination with two-wheeled vehicles and all things mechanical. It was during his four-year stretch in the US Air Force, while stationed in Alaska, he unearthed a musical passion and taught himself guitar and bass guitar. This inspired a desire to be a rock star. The fraction of a penny that he earns from his streaming royalties, coupled with the monumental success of his first book, *Small Portions Café*, have allowed him to stop complaining about the price of a cup of coffee and devote himself fully to his consuming interest in getting his furnace-whisperer license.

When he's not writing, he's likely doing handyman repairs at his home, bicycling or hiking with his wife, practicing bass guitar or cooking a delicious, healthy meal. Doug lives in random parts of the world with his wife, Suzan, and their very cool dog, Juno.

Doug has written and recorded over 75 upbeat, quirky, fun indie rock songs under the artist name Lucky Doug Fergus. His music can be found on all digital platforms. To learn more, please visit www.luckydougpress.com.